THE FAMILY IN A
CHANGING WORLD

THE FAMILY IN A
CHANGING WORLD

Rev. Robert L. Hurley
B.A., M.Div., Ms. (Ed)

Library of Congress Control Number:		2011901620
ISBN:	Hardcover	978-1-4568-6259-6
	Softcover	978-1-4568-6258-9
	Ebook	978-1-4568-6260-2

This book was printed in the United States of America.

To order additional copies of this book, contact:
Xlibris Corporation
1-888-795-4274
www.Xlibris.com
Orders@Xlibris.com
92911

CONTENTS

ACKNOWLEDGMENTS

Sincere and grateful appreciation is extended to Karen King, who spent many hours in editing, transcribing, and typing the original manuscript, and to John and Lula Gray, without whose devotion of time and computer expertise, the arrangement of the text into print-ready format would have been impossible.

And finally, I must pay well-deserved tribute to the hundreds of persons over the past fifty years who have imparted to me a maturing understanding of the meaning of life, and shared with me so much of the triumph and tragedy of daily living.

THE FAMILY IN A CHANGING WORLD

An Overview

This study on the family begins with paraphrased lines from a hit rock and roll song from the sixties by Bob Dylan, in the social and cultural furor following the English invasion of Beatle-Mania: "Come, fathers and mothers from throughout the land, for your sons and your daughters are beyond your command . . . and don't criticize what you can't understand, for the times, they are a'changing." May I suggest to you, that those lines could not have been more profoundly prophetic.

The study presented here is not an academic treatise; indeed, a disciplined effort has been made to avoid the use of technical language. Most families have some grasp of the energy inherent in the family system, but in many cases they do not have sufficient understanding to exercise control over family interaction. This study is presented as a reference for young persons who are seeking relevant material to guide developing relationships, and for more mature couples who are trying to cope with the complexities of family life in a changing world.

This work has evolved from a lifelong interest in the principles of family relationships and gleaned from many years in the pastoral ministry, as well as in the practice of family counseling. This interest has been sharpened through careful observation of the family system, and the emergence of a host of new stresses in the family through the dramatic increase in single-parent and stepfamily relationships.

No discussion of family life would be complete without reference to the dramatic increase in the divorce rate over the past thirty years. Divorce has been a reality for many years, but it was rare before the social excesses of the sixties and the seventies, when it was largely confined to the wealthy and upper-class people. Up until World War II, divorce was almost nonexistent among working class people where it was looked upon with a high degree of social stigma.

However, all of that has changed with breathtaking swiftness through the sexual revolution and the influence upon women by the feminist movement, and as a result of these radical changes, the divorce rate has been hovering near fifty percent over the past quarter century. The impact on family life through these radical social changes has been disastrous and revolutionary, and two generations of innocent children have been traumatized. The politically correct line has been that children from broken homes compared favorably with children reared in stable homes. After years of experience, we realize now that this was little more than wishful thinking, and therapists are now trying diligently to salvage uncounted thousands of young lives—children who were traumatized and scarred by the loss of parents and the disruption of family life at an age in their development when they were most vulnerable.

As reported in the *Baltimore Sun*, a recent study called "The National Marriage Project," Dr. David Popenoe, a Sociology Professor at Rutgers University, wrote: "Where children are living in a loosely-connected and regularly-changing version of the American family, where their parents were never married or they are divorced, and when both parents can be expected to change partners, this has a severe economic effect on the children." Dr. Popenoe said that he was alarmed by the emotional impact on children. "All of us need close relationships to be human, to give life meaning, and to have a feeling of security. It is these close relationships that are in short supply. If your relationships are breaking up all of the time, there is a poverty of connectedness."

According to the report, single young adults not only do not view marriage as a prerequisite for having children, they do not view child rearing as a primary reason to get married.

The study also revealed some startling statistics. Over one-third of children today are born outside of marriage, and nearly seventy percent of children are expected to spend some time with cohabiting adults. The number of children living apart from their biological fathers has doubled over the past four decades, going from seventeen percent in 1960 to thirty-four percent in 2000. Nearly seventy percent of Americans disagree with the statement that the main purpose of marriage is to have children. As a result of the above, Americans are having fewer children, and the combined effects of these demographics are profound. Within families and communities today, and into the future, adults are less likely to be living with children, neighborhoods are less likely to contain children, and children are less likely to be a presence in daily life." The study then offers the conclusion that "children are being pushed to the margins of society, and except when they commit mayhem, to the sidelines of our social conscience."

Many of these stresses on family life are not new; indeed, many are as old as the family itself, dating back to our earliest history. Consider the sibling rivalry of twins, Jacob and Esau, in which the narrative in the Old Testament suggests that their rivalry began even before they were born, and it persisted into their adult lives. Additional interesting family data may be found in a careful study of their family system as it developed in the lives of Jacob and his wives, two of whom were sisters, Leah and Rachel.

While familial stresses are as old as human emotions, their occurrence in our day has been magnified by the unprecedented level of divorce, leading to two or three marriages ending in divorce during the childbearing years. This has led to "Brady Bunches" of yours, mine, and ours. Once they were the exception, but now they seem to be the rule. In one local suburban school, it was found that 80% of the children enrolled were from broken homes. This is the price tag of the social irresponsibility of the past three decades.

The first sweeping change in the dynamics of the family occurred during the War years, from 1940 through 1945, when large numbers of men were called into military service. With the urgent demands of the war effort, our defense industries were progressively forced to turn to women to meet production needs. This led to the familiar figure of "Rosie, the Riveter," and for the first time in our history, a large percentage of our women were employed in the public sector.

A second tidal wave of change in our culture developed with the Hippie era, and the Flower Children of the '60s and '70s. This era was characterized by an organized effort to deny all forms of restraint and responsibility, reject all institutional authority, and "Do one's own thing."

A line from a popular rock and roll band of the time, "Blood, Sweat, and Tears," demanded "Just one thing I ask, don't put no chains on me." This may well have been the mantra of the times. It was a wholesale declaration of independence. The age-old work ethic in our country was largely rejected, the natural spirit of rebellion of youth was given free rein, and all of the above were enthusiastically exploited by M.T.V. in their enticement of youth.

The result of these national trends was the widespread disruption of family life, and Pied Piper wanderlust infected a whole generation of youth and young adults. My wife and I went on a 10,000-mile tour of the country in 1970, and a vivid memory of that trip occurred in California, where we saw a young girl of seventeen or eighteen standing on a corner. When she noted just the two of us in a large sedan, she held up a cardboard sign with the heartbreaking plea, "Anywhere, please."

An interesting comment on that period was made recently by an aging hippie, who said, "In that day, we took what we wanted, and now we no longer want what we took." This era also saw the first major change in the family system, with the establishment of communal households with no regard for family relationships. The sexual revolution was well under way in that period and this led to a sharp increase in teen pregnancies. Also, Roe vs. Wade made abortion legal, which opened the floodgates to a vast and continuing incidence of abortions. At the same time, there has been a growing social tolerance of couples living together without the benefits (or hindrances) of marriage, a relationship without commitment or responsibility. The social changes were revolutionary in this country, and they have led collectively to a radical redefinition of the family.

Until the recent past, the nuclear family was composed of a father, mother, and one or more children. The extended family included in-laws, grandparents, uncles, aunts, and cousins. Today, the family is defined as any two or more persons living together in community, including two males or two females, young couples (male, female, or mixed), as well as aging couples who may live together simply for companionship or for economic reasons.

As one may expect, this cultural phenomenon has introduced a whole new set of social problems. I recently officiated at a wedding in which the bride had three mothers who were to be formally seated! We now have men under forty who are providing child support for three sets of children, and the economic hardships imposed has led to an astounding level of 75% to 80% of women under forty who are now in the workforce, outside of the home. These unprecedented social trends have brought complex changes in the family system and a high level of stress, particularly among women who must balance the demands of being a full-time wife and mother, and the requirements of a full-time job in the public sector, or a career in business or industry, often necessitating long hours in the workplace, or that work must be brought home.

No survey of family life today would be complete without some reference to the impact of homosexuality on the family, and the implications the national homosexual agenda may hold for the family. It is not uncommon today to have a father or mother announce to their family that they have become gay and desert years of relationships. Yet, gay activists have always longed for family status, and they have worked diligently to attain it.

Thirty years ago, homosexual couples were legally prohibited from adoption. Faced with this formidable legal obstacle, they devised an "end run" by which pregnancy was achieved through artificial insemination. When the baby was born, they now had a child; therefore, they were a family. A second route was brought about by women becoming homosexual who were married and had one or more children. Through this natural process, they were also a family. As a result of these effective strategies, along with a progressive toleration by the culture and by the courts, many states now permit adoption by homosexual couples, male as well as female.

A further impetus in their quest for legal status as a family has been derived by the successful effort by homosexual activists to link the homosexual agenda to the Civil Rights movement, championed so successfully by Dr. Martin Luther King. In their view, all legal or cultural limits imposed on homosexuality are declared to be a form of discrimination against a victimized social minority. This long-range effort has proved to be quite successful.

In addition to the national drive for legal family status through the courts, the gay community has long recognized that until they can achieve cultural validation, their claims will remain legalistic and limited. Therefore, they have turned the national spotlight on the churches, with progressively more strident demands for some form of spiritually sanctioned marriage. Since the Catholic Church is monolithic and totally opposed to any form of homosexual activity, the gay activists have focused their attention on the more moderate Protestant denominations.

As a result of finding themselves driven by very public demands into a defensive posture, virtually all of the major Protestant denominations have been "studying" the concerns of homosexuality for the past thirty years. A thoughtful person may ask why we have this divisive and protracted exercise in futility. Primarily, it may be seen as a philosophic "Catch 22," by which there is little to be gained and much to be lost, through any public conclusion.

In considering this, I am reminded of a favorite story from the columnist, Ann Landers. A lady wrote that she had attended a black-tie diplomatic dinner in Washington, where she had been seated by a foreign diplomat. She had been so impressed by his encyclopedic knowledge and his suave demeanor that she had thoughtlessly taken a sip of hot coffee. As an embarrassed result, she asked Miss Landers what was the least damaging solution to her dilemma. Ann Landers' reply was a classic that I have never forgotten. "I am a little uncertain as to what Amy Vanderbilt might advise in this situation, but I can assure you, as a practical woman of the world, of this fact. When you take a sip of coffee that is too hot, the next thing that you do will be wrong."

This is an oblique answer to the quandary of the churches in their study of homosexuality. If they would issue any judgment critical of homosexuality, they would be loudly and publicly labeled as bigoted and homophobic. However, if they were to express any level of approval of homosexuality as an alternative lifestyle, there would be an exodus from that denomination that would make the Exodus under Moses seem like small peanuts in comparison. Consequently, the studies will continue.

As a result of these social trends, the most serious erosion of the family has been the institution of marriage itself. Prior to World War II, most females were married by the age of eighteen, and an unmarried woman in her twenties was often (privately if not publicly) considered to be an "Old Maid." Today, most couples are delaying marriage until the mid-twenties or later, and since many people approaching marriage have themselves been the product of a broken home, they tend to think of divorce as a common option. As a consequence of these social and cultural tends, the marriage liturgy had been subtly modified in their minds, from the traditional, "As long as you both shall live," to the modern version, "As long as you both shall love."

It is difficult to interpret this alarming erosion of marriage as anything less than destructive to a treasured institution, and ultimately damaging to family life as well. In the book of Genesis, the book of Beginnings, it is written: "So God created Man in His own image, in His own image He created Him and male and female He created them. And God blessed them and said, "Be fruitful and multiply . . . Therefore, shall a man leave his father and mother and cleave unto his wife, and they shall be no more twain (two), but one flesh." As some wag has observed, "In the beginning, God created Adam and Eve, not Adam and Steve."

CHAPTER ONE:

The Early Years In The Family

The popular ditty tells us that "Love and marriage, love and marriage—they go together like a horse and carriage," but where does love begin? Despite what young persons may believe, you cannot make love, indeed, you cannot even know what love is until you have experienced it. Again, love does not just happen; it must be developed out of a lasting relationship.

Let it be said unequivocally that the people who are the most successful in building relationships with others are those who are most secure within themselves. That security can only be developed and nurtured in a home environment where children learned the meaning of love by being loved unconditionally.

In the mystery of creation, God made men and women to be different, and the difference is far deeper than the reality of different plumbing. While lines have been blurred in the recent past, men and women have different roles in life, beginning with the reality that the Creator endowed women with the creative ability to conceive and give birth to children. As a result of that uniqueness, the parallel relationship of fathers to their children and mothers to their children is not only not the same, it is not even similar. A man may become a father and never know it, but if a woman becomes pregnant and does not realize it, some helpful soul will be kind enough to tell her.

The traditional role of the father has been that of the breadwinner and the security of the family, and the mender of broken things, while the role of the mother has been the emotional security of the family, and the mender of broken hearts. However, one of the most hopeful developments in the family system in recent years has been the substantial increase in the involvement of fathers in the day to care for their children. The design of the Creator was that every child must have two parents, a father as well as a mother. Thankfully, this is much more of a reality in this new generation of fathering.

The next critical issue in the family system is that of gender. Little girls learn the meaning of femininity and the arts of being female from their mothers. Likewise, boys find their role model in being a male from their fathers. Beginning in early childhood in the home, in childcare, and in kindergarten, boys and girls play together and interact with one another with little or no regard to gender; but in elementary school, the genders begin to gravitate together, and through most of the preteen years, girls and boys are largely separated by their own instinctive choices. At about the age of twelve, tentative awareness of the opposite sex and the interaction between boys and girls becomes more apparent.

It should be noted that in terms of maturity, both physical and emotional, girls begin to move ahead of boys in the preteen years, and this differentiation continues through the teen years. When a boy first begins to "notice" a girl at this stage, it is often expressed in the form of teasing. This tentative form of interrelationship continues in a progressive manner through home parties, class trips, group visits to the movies, and preteen dances.

In the early teen years, this growing opposite sex attraction is enhanced by house parties, walking together in school hallways, and "cruising" in the malls. For most girls in this age group, sleepovers in the homes of friends become one of the most active interests, and of course, the main topic of all-night conversation is boys. As the teenagers progress through the high school years, the interaction grows in a predictable sequence beginning with group activities such as dances, parties, and group jaunts to the movies with pairing off becoming more prevalent.

By age sixteen, when most boys and girls take Driver's Ed and get their driver's license and possibly their first car, the dating game begins in earnest. Often parents with teens at this age will only allow double dating, but in the fierce resistance of son or daughter, this stricture is soon abandoned and the dating gains more momentum. In most cases, by the junior or senior years in high school, most teens will encounter their first experience of "puppy love."

It is in this period that the dynamics of the family begin to affect the teen in significant ways, for it is in the home that patterns of communication are formed and gender patterns of interaction become more fixed. If the father is the "King of the Hill" type, who exerts a high level of control in the family structure, the oldest son will probably follow in his path. Likewise, if the mother is controlling and demanding, the oldest daughter tends to follow in this pattern. If the mother manages to control the family through tactics of manipulation, this subtle style will be noted and emulated by her daughters.

CHAPTER TWO:

Family Alliances

At this point in examining family dynamics, it is helpful to note the typical patterns they tend to follow. Although there are exceptions, these patterns tend to be cross-gender. The father is often the first love of the daughter, and her relationship with her father becomes a strong unconscious influence in her later relationships with men. Likewise, the mother becomes the first love object for boys, and that relationship also is a strong influence in his later choices in dating and in a mate. In part, this cross-gender alliance is also related to the separation process, in which the daughter must rebel against her mother, and the son must declare independence from his father.

This process is often difficult for parents to understand. I have seen examples, in which a daughter and her mother were so close up to the age of twelve, that if the daughter's nose itched, the mother would sneeze! Then, progressively, and often inexplicably from the mother's perspective, the daughter becomes more rebellious and difficult to understand, sometimes to the extreme extent that by the age of fourteen, the daughter would disagree with her mother about the time, if they were both looking at the same clock!

Because of the close and untroubled relationship that they enjoyed before puberty, many mothers make the mistake of concluding that the rebellion of their daughters is personal, done out of spite or a deliberate attempt to hurt their mother. This may occur, but in my experience, it is rarely true. In part, the driving force is hormonal, coinciding with the onset of the menstrual cycle, but it is also a natural part of the developmental process, in which the daughter becomes separated from her mother, and the son is separated from his father.

It is important to note that it is at this point that the cross-gender relationship becomes critical. In the separation stresses of the daughter, the father is not directly involved in the personality conflict between the daughter and her mother. As a result, the daughter is encouraged to turn to her father for the emotional support that she cannot accept from her mother at that time. In a similar manner, the mother is not directly involved in the emotional conflict between father and son, except as a referee. This makes it possible for the son to turn to his mother for emotional resources that he cannot accept at that time from his father.

Because it is so personally painful to them, the parents sometimes fail to understand that the separation process is just as painful, and often as confusing, to the teen as well as to the parents. I have often observed that the love, support, and understanding of the opposite gender parent is so important to the teen, both consciously and unconsciously, in the painful process of separation, that deep emotional bonds may be formed with the opposite gender parent that continue throughout the life of both the parent and the child.

In my own family, the conflict between my father and my oldest brother was probably more intense than most, and as a consequence, my mother was more protective and sheltering of him throughout her life. I was standing by her bed when she died at eighty-three, and her last conscious thought was for his welfare.

Similarly, gender may play a critical role in terms of the birth and sequence of children. In one case, a couple encountered fertility problems. The husband desperately wanted a son, and after several years of clinical intervention, the wife became pregnant and gave birth to a daughter. The disappointment of the father was so painful that an unusual reaction transpired. As nearly as biology would permit, the father became the mother. He provided almost all of the care for the child; he dressed her as a boy and took her with him wherever he went, as well as in his chores and tasks around the home. It was common for her to come in with her father covered in dirt and grime, and perhaps even grease. The gender reversal was made even more drastic in that she spent almost no time with her mother drying dishes, setting the table, making cookies, or other common female skills. Insofar as it was physically possible, the father turned the little girl into the boy that he had always wanted.

This unusual state of affairs was further complicated by the subsequent birth of the second child, another daughter. Having effectively lost her first daughter, the mother's attachment to the second child was fiercely protective, and with the opposite effect, that the child spent virtually no time with her father. The clinical picture was further complicated by the fact that the new daughter was petite, beautiful, and very feminine. As a result of these factors, there was a constant and negative contrast between the new daughter and her scruffy, tomboyish sister.

These conditions remained largely unchanged until the older daughter came into puberty. This startling development shattered her illusion that she was a boy. Since there were no more children, her beautiful sister remained the baby and a daily reminder of all that she could never be. The father did not know how to cope with this situation, and she had no emotional bond with her mother. All of these factors converged upon the child as a harsh reminder that she was not a boy, but she had no clue or incentive as to how to become a girl. This tragic dilemma brought the onset of mental illness. Through her teen years, her mental state deteriorated further into psychosis, and her adult years have been almost totally spent in psychiatric institutions.

CHAPTER THREE:

The Dating Game

With this essential background, we may now turn to the dating game. During this period, only in part because of the separation process, the perspective of parents and teens becomes very different. For the parents, it is the necessity to maintain some degree of parental control. For the teens, the most powerful dynamic during the teen years is peer pressure. All studies have concluded that at this stage of life, the acceptance and approval of their peer group is much more important to teens than the approval of their parents. The basic conflict between parents and their adolescent children arises from the need of parents to set limits and the progressive demands by the teenagers for more freedom. In this arena, the cards are stacked against the parents, since the primary sources of information at this stage in their development are from the youth culture, and in even greater measure from M.T.V. This giant media shaper of young lives originated with the mania generated by the Beatles, and, in its explosive growth since, has deliberately exploited the naturally rebellious nature of youth, from age ten (or younger) up through the high school. This has been accomplished through a heady mixture of the primary interests of adolescents—alcohol, drugs, and sex, and all of this through an unholy alliance between business and entertainment. M.T.V. has become the major medium for merchandising to youth, with billions in potential sales.

In the saturated sexual climate of today, it is not surprising to discover that recent studies indicate that seventy-five to eighty percent of high school seniors are sexually active. Some girls have reported that their first sexual experience began by the age of twelve. These statistics are a stark reminder of the extent of the sexual revolution. It has become common practice for many parents to allow their son or daughter to entertain a boyfriend or girlfriend in their bedroom, and it is not unusual today for parents to allow a live-in companion for their son or daughter in their home. Another factor in this equation is seen in the large number of latchkey children who are home, often totally unsupervised, from 2:30 or 3:00 o'clock until one of the parents arrives home at 5:30. Given the sexually charged climate in which these young persons must grow up today, this one single factor is a formula for disaster.

A critical element in this problem arises from a fact of creation. Most girls are sexually mature by the age of twelve or thirteen, but they do not have the emotional maturity to understand the meaning of sex until they are eighteen or older. This quirk of nature leads to a period of five or six years when there is considerable temptation to play with fire, with a totally inadequate grasp of the powerful stresses involved, or the ultimate consequences of the choices they are making.

Another complication, in the dating game today, is the common practice of boys and girls moving in together, often quite early in their relationship, sometimes before they are twenty. This ushers in the complexity of sexual tensions before the emotional bonds and the level of commitment have matured to the point of adult responsibility. An objective observer may be led to wonder, how have we come to where we are? Part of the answer must be seen in the social and cultural evolution of our times. Most of the parents of these young adults today grew up in the chaos of the sixties and the seventies—a time when virtually all forms of restraint were denied.

If an unplanned pregnancy occurs, then the couple is faced with a critical choice—whether to terminate the pregnancy through abortion, a traumatic event that may, and often does, leave permanent scars in the soul of the girl. Girls in this unfortunate situation are led by their peers, or even professional counselors, to believe that this solution to the problem is common and that it no longer carries any stigma (who is to know about it?), and it will soon be forgotten by everyone. However, somewhere along the line, they find that they have been misled. They remember the date, and wonder what the child may have looked like. Was it a boy or a girl? Such thoughts may become an agonizing concern with no one with whom they may share the pain. The alternative choice is to accept the responsibility to make a joint commitment in a relationship that may not be secure enough to deal with the physical and emotional demands posed by a new baby.

Additionally, the fact of a pregnancy raises complex questions, particularly for an unmarried couple. If the decision is made to bring the child to birth, the female often feels insecure and vulnerable; out of this sense of urgency, she presses for marriage. While the prospective father may feel some anxiety about the relationship and the legal and moral implications for the future, all too often he just walks away, leaving the young mother-to-be to cope with the situation alone.

Another unfortunate alternative often faced by young teenage girls who become pregnant is the pressure by parents, and often by social workers, in the suggestion that she put the baby up for adoption, stressing the likelihood that the child will have a better life with an adoptive family. For most sixteen—to eighteen-year-old girls this is probably accurate. However, this fails to consider the emotional trauma imposed upon the girl, who will remember forever the baby's name and his/her birthday. She will wonder what the baby looks like on the first birthday, and what it may have felt like as the youngster got on the bus for the first day of school. These are some of the thoughts expressed to me by these women, perhaps years later. So we realize that a decision like this is relatively easy to make—for everyone but the mother.

One of the constant topics raised in counseling, with teens or in group discussions about dating, is the question of control in the inevitable process of "making out," particularly with girls. How far can one go? How far should one go? The consensus seems to be that this decision should never be made in the pressure of an overheated moment, but rather in the shower, or in the relative calm of preparing for the date. A second reality to keep in mind in this context is the tendency of boys (and sometimes girls) to expect the level of intimacy on this date to begin at the place where the last date ended, and this is coupled with the natural tendency to move farther into unexplored experience with each subsequent date.

Unless some constraint and control are exercised in these dating experiences, the end result may be too much and too soon. I fear today that some mothers may set up a young daughter for such premature pressure by permitting (or even encouraging) her in the use of more mature forms of makeup, as well as in the practice of dressing in provocative and sexy attire. In a similar vein, it is not unusual for parents to allow, or even to arrange, house parties for young teens without adult supervision.

Seen in total perspective, there seems to be considerable pressure today for our children and youth to grow up too fast. How many times have you heard the expression, often from a parent, "She is fourteen going on twenty?" The wisdom of the Book of Ecclesiastes comes to mind, "He (God) has made everything beautiful in its time." We can sympathize with the fact that a boy of twelve does not believe that he will live long enough to get his driver's license. However, a boy or girl will only be fourteen once, and my advice to teens, and to their parents, is to treasure the moments, because they are too soon gone. A line from one of Frank Sinatra's great hits has an important word for teens, "Let's just take it nice and easy, and make all the stops along the way."

TIPS FOR TEENAGERS

It may be appropriate to offer some tips for teenagers for the dating game:

1. Date only boys or girls in your appropriate age group. A fourteen-year-old girl dating an eighteen-year-old boy is a sure formula for disaster.
2. Never date a person that you would not want to marry.
3. Be very thoughtful about interracial and interreligious relationships. These can lead to almost insolvable family problems later in life.
4. Famous last words, "Oh, I know that he is a little wild and crazy now, but he will settle down after we are married." It almost never happens.
5. The Creator has endowed many young persons with a "rescuer" personality. This signals danger ahead, particularly in regard to alcohol and drug addiction. Such attempts at rescue are rarely, if ever, successful.
6. Never allow yourself to be drawn into a situation that you cannot control.

7. Be very cautious about riding in a car with other teens, particularly when the driver has been drinking. The #1 cause of death among teenage youth is in auto accidents. I lost a very talented and promising nephew who was riding in a car with a teenage driver who was driving too fast, and slid into a pole on a curve.
8. Never drink and drive, and never ride in a car with a driver who has been drinking.
9. Young persons should never attend a house party without adult supervision. Parents should check this out before giving permission to attend. Another factor to investigate is to insure that no alcohol will be available.

COURTSHIP AND THE ENGAGEMENT

I believe that many young people have not thought of it in this way, but the dating experience is an important part of the process of maturing. The couple that meets in middle school, dates through high school and college, and then gets married, never having seriously dated any other person, is a distinct minority. Or to express it in another way, the first person that you date is rarely the person you will marry.

Dating is a process of selection and comparison, and to shorten the process is to invite making a wrong choice. It has been reflected in many studies that girls will often unconsciously look for a man who is like their father; and boys, too often, are looking for a mother instead of a wife. An element of insurance in this experience is to have dated enough individuals so that you have mature judgment when you meet the right person.

As another caution, love at first sight sounds very romantic, but it seldom happens that way. I have known happily married couples who said that their first impression in meeting each other was something less than favorable, or perhaps even negative. However, serious dating with the right person brings a progressive sense, not only of attraction, but involvement in each other's lives and a growing feeling of incompleteness when you are apart.

As love matures, the time comes when the kiss at the door at midnight no longer satisfies, when your love for each other demands expression, and one or the other initiates what both are feeling. The next step is the proposal with the presenting of the ring, signifying formal engagement.

These events reflect the beginning of plans for the wedding, and the laying of the foundations for a permanent relationship.

I have noted couples in counseling who asked how long the engagement should be, and there is no certain answer for that question. The great majority of couples will be married within a year, or certainly within two years, but often the question revolves around problems that need to be resolved and logistical complications with the multitude of arrangements needed for the wedding, many of which are time-consuming.

A logical question arises as to the purpose or value of the engagement period. When the decision to wed is finalized, this raises important questions that need to be resolved relative to the relationship. This may involve communication, or finances, or further discussion relative to a projected family, but the engagement provides the opportunity to begin in earnest the process of adjustment that will be continued in the early years of marriage. It is also during this period that the issue of control may surface. When conflict arises, the issue of control should be recognized and addressed. Basically, control will be an issue in every relationship, but it may also pose a serious problem.

Under most circumstances, the dating game has an ultimate ending, usually in the setting of an engagement. This is the beginning of a commitment that leads to marriage. Its duration is highly variable, from a few days to a few years, and in a few instances, to a bride-to-be who wonders if it will ever end in marriage! However, this period is very important in the deepening relationship that leads to marriage and in making plans for the wedding, which is the next step in the family scene.

CHAPTER FOUR:

The Wedding

The next sequential step in the life of the family, after the dating game, is the wedding. Most brides will tell you that planning the wedding is the most stressful experience they had previously encountered. The most helpful advice I can give to young couples is that they basically have two choices—either to run the wedding or the wedding will run them!

When the date for the wedding has been set, it is imperative to select the setting as soon as possible. If you elect to be married in a church or other religious institution, contact the pastor or other religious leader to clear the date. If the location is a church, this will usually determine who will officiate. If this is not the case, then it will be necessary to clear the date and time with the pastor, priest, rabbi, or other person who will perform the ceremony.

With these arrangements made, the selection of the facility for the reception becomes critical since the most popular sites for receptions are in great demand, especially in peak periods such as early summer, and in some cases, the date must be set a year or more in advance. Also, it is helpful to make an early selection of a photographer, for some of the same reasons, for those who are well-known are also busy. Be advised that this is a fairly expensive item in planning for the wedding, and some couples elect to use an amateur photographer who has good equipment and is known to be proficient in using it. Often, these albums are comparable to a professional layout, and considerably less expensive.

Since the photography is such a crucial and important and permanent memento of your wedding, it is helpful to ask for a review of the photographer's work before you sign the contract. A fine set of photographs is essential for your wedding, and there is only one opportunity. I recall one wedding in which an amateur photographer made a full set of wedding pictures using a viewfinder camera, and then discovered that he had forgotten to remove the lens cap!

When the wedding announcement is made in the society section of your newspaper, you may receive one or more calls from a wedding manager. This is a business developed in the past few years by which, for a fee, they will plan and manage every detail of your wedding, including the wedding ceremony. These services are growing rapidly in popularity, and the weddings at which I have officiated where these services were utilized were very well done. In general, the preparation for the wedding is the most tedious and frustrating, largely because of the myriad details that demand your attention. However, most brides will tell you, in retrospect, that the most difficult and irritating concerns are not the physical arrangements, or the wedding details, but the management of relationships.

Again, the most vexing issues seem to surround the bride, her mother, and the mother of the groom. Since the bride's family traditionally pays the lion's share of the cost of the wedding, the bride's father may become an important factor in the equation. The best advice that I can give to brides is that, despite all of the aggravation, just keep your cool, and do not allow these distractions to dim your excitement. Listen as respectfully as circumstances will permit to all of the counsel (which you probably don't need), then finally, do what seems best to you, because it is YOUR wedding!

With all of the minute details required in planning a wedding, it seems clear to me that one of the most urgent issues is often neglected, and sometimes forgotten, and that is the need for competent marriage counseling. In many cases, the couple spends far more time in planning the wedding, an event which will be over in two or three days, than they invest in preparation for a marriage, a commitment and a relationship that are expected to endure for a lifetime.

It is necessary only to examine the record, indicating that approximately half of all current marriages will end in divorce, to understand the critical need for a thorough and comprehensive preparation for marriage. All states require extensive training and a test covering a broad range of legal and practical driving knowledge and skills before a driver's license is awarded; yet, there are no regulations that require counseling before marriage.

The first observation that we may make is that the interests and qualifications of the minister, priest, rabbi, or other person who may be officiating will vary widely. This raises the question relative to marriage counseling as to both the number of sessions and the material to be covered. What is the nature of good counseling, and what is the content to be explored? There are excellent materials available in every good library, and it will reward any couple planning marriage to invest some time in researching these resources. However it is obtained, and from whatever sources, marriage counseling should include the following areas. A complete family history should be conducted for both parties, since most of our values are formed in the family of origin.

1. An extensive personality profile should be made for each partner. Is he/she:

    a. Optimistic or pessimistic?
    b. Suspicious by nature or trusting?
    c. Greedy or generous? A giver or a taker?
    d. Moody or cheerful?
    e. Dominating or submissive?
    f. Aggressive or passive?
    g. Jealous and possessive or understanding and sharing?
    h. A responsible person or undisciplined in his/her habits?
    i. Vindictive and judgmental or forgiving in nature?
    j. Perfectionistic or hanging loose?
    k. Anxious and tense or relaxed and casual?

These personality traits may be explored and used as a catalyst for dialogue.

2. Communication is a critical issue in every marriage. The counselor should explore the patterns of communication in each family of origin and in each partner. Also important to observe: Is each a good listener?

3. What are the hopes and dreams, the aims and goals of each partner? Secondly, are these marriage goals mutually compatible?

4. What are the hopes and expectations in regard to children? Are these family plans acceptable to both parties? Explore and resolve any differences.

5. Was a strong tendency to control evident in the father or mother of either mate? The issue of control is one of the major problems in marriage, and the pattern learned in the home tends to perpetuate itself.

6. Money is the #1 marriage problem over the nation, and it remains one of the most common sources of conflict in every marriage. Explore the attitudes toward money in each family of origin and with each mate. Also under this topic, consider the financial status of both bride and groom, particularly in the use of credit cards. How much credit card debt is owed collectively?

7. Examine the in-law relationships on both sides, for these are the most important four people in the world for these young persons for many years to come. Yet, these relationships are a common source of conflict, particularly if the separation process has not been completely resolved for either the bride or the groom.

8. Following money, sex is the second most serious area of conflict for every marriage. This may seem a bit strange, since we live in the most sex-saturated culture since ancient Rome, yet many couples have little knowledge of the physical and emotional dynamics of sexual experience. The following are topics that should be considered in sexual counseling.

   a. Men and women are different, and it isn't just a matter of different plumbing. Men are willing to express love in order to get sex, while women often are willing to accept sex in order to obtain love.

   b. Men reach a sexual peak early, at around 20, while women mature more slowly, reaching a sexual peak at about 30. These normal differences can be a source of conflict.

   c. Another critical factor is the sex drive itself. Many people do not know that the sex drive is fixed. It is a part of our genetic inheritance, and it cannot be changed. In extremes, a man may need sex four or five times a week, or he may become mildly interested in sex once a month. In most cases, the needs of husband and wife are similar, and differences easily accommodated. However, it is not unusual for these differences to become a problem. In most such cases, sexual therapy will help to resolve the differences.

d. The next area of concern may be sexual arousal. For purposes of contrast, a man may be sexually aroused in 30 seconds, from a cold start, while the same process for a female may take 30 minutes. For a male, sexual arousal is largely physical, but for a woman, it is largely emotional. As some women complain, about the time when the wife is becoming mildly interested in what is happening—it isn't. With any evidence of sexual dysfunction, your family doctor can rule out any physical problem, and for other sexual issues, a sex therapist can usually be helpful.

THE ADJUSTMENT PERIOD

The years immediately following the wedding are years of adjustment. These personal resolutions of conflict are an inevitable part of the beginning of marriage. These accommodations begin with the experience of living together, when little differences that were unnoticed before now become apparent. Such adjustments begin with obvious differences such as our biological clock. Many persons are day people, while many others are night people. Some are acclimated to getting up at the crack of dawn, while others, if they are free to follow their inclinations, may begin to stir about 9:30 AM. Differences in our choices of food, or even in the preparation of food, may become an immediate concern. Some of the more difficult adjustments may be in our habits of life. One partner may be a neatnik, while the other may tend to be a slob.

An observant marriage counselor may discover some of the more abrasive differences in the counseling sessions before marriage, but many of the less noticeable personality traits do not become apparent until the young couple is living together. Does the groom have skills in cooking? Has he been trained in the home to share in the household chores such as cleaning or doing the laundry? In my case, I grew up in a home with seven sisters, and I did more work in the house by accident than I did on purpose.

Many men have been conditioned to expect that the daily work in the home is women's work, but when the wife spends the same number of hours at her work as her husband, obviously some sharing of the work in the home is needed out of fairness, if not out of a caring concern to lessen the burdens of the wife. One observation may be helpful at this point—that ingrained habits or ways of relating may be difficult to change; therefore, a careful survey of the home of origin may be revealing.

One of the first conflicts to arise in most early marriages is that of in-law relationships. This area is almost certain to become problematic if the separation process has been incomplete or inadequate. Often the difficulty arises through dependency. The father of the groom is constantly finding things to do in which the son is expected to do the work indicated, or to provide needed assistance. Experience would indicate, however, that emotional dependency is more commonly the culprit. The bride must call her mother each day of the honeymoon, or the groom is expected to come back home three or four times a week.

Often such stress surfaces when one or the other set of parents forms the habit of dropping in unannounced at regular intervals, or if they live farther away, they come for visits expecting to stay several days. Additionally, some parents feel entitled to meddle in the affairs of the young couple, sometimes in grossly inappropriate ways.

However, we must realize that all of the joking comments about mothers-in-law are just that—they are jokes. In reality, the great majority of in-laws are caring, concerned, and often the best friends the young couple will ever have. In any case, these four older adults will usually be the most important resource people will find in the next twenty-five years, available to them in dozens of practical daily ways. In view of these factors, it is critically important for the new family to have the best possible relations with their in-laws.

CHAPTER FIVE:

Pregnancy And The Nest-Building Years

The first three years of marriage are considered to be an adjustment period, a time when basic conflicts are resolved, the pressure points in the relationship are smoothed out, differing needs are brought into harmony, and family relationships are worked out. It is often in this period that the first pregnancy occurs. Hopefully, there has been time enough for the relationship to become comfortable and secure, for pregnancy ushers in a whole new set of dynamics. While it is the wife that is pregnant, it will profoundly affect every part of their life together.

While the physical changes in pregnancy tend to dominate, the emotional factors are more difficult to manage. Occasional irritability may occur, and the wife may feel that there is some lack of understanding on the husband's part, if for no other reason than that it is she that is pregnant, and there is no way that he can walk in her shoes. Hormonal changes may bring mood swings, and there may be strange yens in terms of the things one craves to eat. Because of the physical changes occurring, there is often a lack of energy and back strain because of the change in weight distribution.

Additionally, when the wife discovers that she is pregnant, there is an unconscious and inescapable tendency to turn inward. The net result of this is that her emotional capital becomes divided, and she cannot devote the lion's share of her attention to her husband, as she has in the past. If the husband is sensitive and emotionally mature, he is able to understand and accept this progressive change with good grace. However, if he tends to be emotionally dependent and self-centered, and needs more attention than most, he may develop an unconscious resentment toward the unborn baby. Without realizing it or understanding it, he blames the pregnancy for the deficits he is experiencing in his inner life. These factors may trigger an unconscious antagonism with child that may persist into adult relationships.

These factors are also related in many cases to a gradual decline in the sex drive of the mother during pregnancy. Since the sex needs of the father remain essentially unchanged, and while he understands and accepts these changes in his wife intellectually, there is at least some sense of change and loss. It should be noted that these adjustments are a normal and expected part of the reality of pregnancy, and the impact that they have in the life of the family. The great majority of young couples accept these challenges and sacrifices gladly as a part of the experience of having a baby and becoming a family, and they grow in maturity through the process.

The final challenge in pregnancy is giving birth. The process is more extended and difficult for a first birth, and this may be one factor in the proliferation of C-sections or Caesarean births. The suspicion persists, however, that the primary cause is the fear by obstetricians of malpractice suits and the alarming rise in the cost of malpractice insurance. This has driven some specialists in the field to leave the practice of obstetrics entirely, requiring some expectant mothers to turn to another obstetrician who may be less experienced.

With all of these things considered, the vast majority of new mothers have a normal delivery and a healthy baby. Only a few years in the past a woman "in confinement" was not permitted to stand or walk for nine days! In contrast, some states have passed legislation requiring HMOs to allow two days in the hospital for new mothers since it had become common practice to discharge a new mother in only twenty-four hours. This practice sends the new mother home when she is unable either to care for herself or the new baby, and often with little knowledge or experience in providing such care. However, the Creator, in His wisdom, has met this need in the invention of grandmothers! Here is the competent woman who, in the trite expression of the times, "Has been there and done that." She knows the needs of the new mother as well as the experience needed to care for the newborn.

Meanwhile, the new parents rejoice in thanksgiving that the long travail of pregnancy has ended, and they actually have a new baby! The first time that you look down upon this wonderful little face, with its unbelievable combination of father and mother (and sometimes, the eyes or nose of a grandparent), you suddenly begin to believe in miracles, and that is the only word that adequately describes the feeling.

Within a week, the new mother is able to care for the new baby, and the proud father has taken over much of the daily routine (or arranged for such assistance as may be needed). There are nights when sleep is interrupted, bouts with the croup, experiences of non-stop crying, and many anxious calls to the pediatrician. Yet, at the same time, each day is a recurring miracle, with the baby beginning to respond to the mother and father, with the first smile and the first laugh. Somewhere between the daily joys and the never-ending needs of a new baby, you begin to feel the overwhelming conviction that this is the meaning and purpose of your existence, this amazing partnership with God in the creation of a new life. There is one urgent word: Treasure these moments, for they pass so swiftly. Before you can turn around (and long before you are ready for it), this little guy or gal will be trudging bravely down the walk to get on the school bus, and you will cry all day because, suddenly, the future is now.

Given the complexity posed by single-parent families, stepfamilies, and teenage mothers, what possibilities are open to us to strengthen the family? I believe that the security and stability of the family begins in the rediscovery and reaffirmation of the sanctity of marriage. The institution of marriage is the crowning gift of a gracious and benevolent God to His people, and it has survived the many forces thrown against it since the dawn of creation. "For this cause shall a man leave the home of his father and his mother, and cleave unto his wife, and they shall be no longer twain (two) but one flesh."

Part of the decision-making process before deciding to start a family begins with a deliberate commitment by both parents that this child, and any others to follow, will be the number #1 priority in this marriage until the youngest child reaches eighteen. This means that all decisions made relating to the family will be made with the intention that the well-being of the children will remain as the primary consideration. With many of the families that I have worked with in the process of divorce over the years, it seemed clear to me that the happiness and well-being of the divorcing parents were the most important factors in the equation. Concern for the emotional security of the children seemed almost like an after-thought, with the hope and expectation that they would adjust to these traumatic events in their lives.

The next need, in my judgment, is to provide young couples with all of the information and resources they need in order for them to be more effective and responsible parents. This will include teaching them how to love their children creatively and unconditionally.

All too often, the message that the children receive is that a father will love his teenage son if he refrains from purple, spiked hair or a Mohawk, and the mother will love her teenage daughter if she will lower the hem of her skirt about ten inches, or if, God forbid, she never even considers a pierced navel!

In the early life of the family, a word of concern needs to be expressed. The vast majority of mothers are now employed outside the home. In part, this is a result of the substantial increase in the percentage of girls who are now college graduates, as compared with an earlier day. These young women naturally expect to reap the benefits of their education through some form of a public career. However, it seems to me that when a married couple decides to start a family, some critical questions should be answered. Given the economics of the family, is it absolutely essential for the mother to work, and if it can be managed economically, even if some sacrifice may be required, should this possibility not be taken into account?

In considering this question, many couples today are taking a hard look and doing the math. In virtually all cases, a second car will be needed, bringing with it the cost of insurance, the high price of gasoline, and normal maintenance. The economy-minded woman will also factor in the extra wardrobe needs of a career in business or industry, the cost of day care and after-school programs her hours may require, and the possible need for some outside help in the home. When all of these collateral costs are summed up, they may conclude that the net income realized is not worth the sacrifices required.

Another critical issue to be considered is that of women's health. It is commonly recognized that the greatest hazard in the emotional well-being of women today is the stress of trying to manage two full-time responsibilities, the increasing stress of a full-time career, and the full-time demands of managing a home, often with one or more children. Many women today are accomplishing this, but they are finding that the physical and emotional price they must pay is higher than they anticipated. Most also recognize that even with highly motivated women with exceptional energy, these dual requirements make it virtually impossible to be fully effective in both arenas.

In considering the stresses on the family, it seems beyond question that the most difficult problem encountered by parents and teens, or preteens, is the breakdown in communication. Clearly, this remains as one of the perennial roadblocks in successful family relationships, and it is only in part related to peer pressure and the inevitable process of separation. One of the important issues for children in this age group, from twelve through sixteen, or later, is the first identity crisis when "self" must be identified on their terms, rather than the terms of their parents. At this age, the mental processes of youth are very keen, although also very inexperienced. This mental acuity leads them to question everything, but their lack of experience often leads to errors in judgment, sometimes quite serious, involving them in risky behavior. This is due in part to the natural recklessness of youth, and also in part, because of their inability to understand and anticipate the consequences of the choices they have made.

Probably the most difficult area of concern between parents and their children is that of communication. Next question—what possibilities do we have to bridge this gap between parents and their children, when the relative positions remain so polarized? The first observation is that most efforts in this area are twelve years too late, hence the purpose of this discussion. The art and skill of the exchange of feelings in this relationship must begin with the emergence of personality at the age of two or three. This has its beginning when the parent involved informs the child that it is bedtime and the toys must be picked up and put away. There are two issues here: The first is that the child is not yet ready for bed at that time, and the second difference of opinion is that the child is not yet ready to pick up his toys. With considerable determination, the child stomps his little foot, looks the parent in the eye, and says an emphatic "NO!" Now the manner in which this conflict of will is resolved may well be the precursor of many such exchanges to come.

In this scenario, the first opportunity for the parent to manage this standoff creatively is to first defuse the encounter by lessening the tension; and secondly, by patiently explaining to the child the necessary reasons for both requests. When some meeting of the minds begins to happen, it may be helpful for the parent to offer to assist in the toy-gathering process, then tuck the child into bed and read a favorite story. This helps to resolve the contest of wills without a damaging defeat for the child, or the need for stern authority on the part of the parent.

However, this initial encounter will provide a heads-up for the parent, for there will be many other such encounters ahead. No two children are the same, and the emergence of a distinct personality will vary from one child to another. It will be apparent early on if this will be an occasional testing of the parent, or if the pattern of rebellion becomes a daily confrontation.

In this situation, you may be dealing with a strong-willed child, and this is a special challenge, requiring additional resources. Many parents faced with this problem have found Dr. James Dobson's book, "The Strong-Willed Child," to be rewarding and helpful. However, there are many other resources available in your local library, and some time spent in seeking the wisdom of experts will provide a wealth of information in handling this problem. The basic solution to this vexing challenge is the art of communication. This is enhanced when the parent takes the time to explain clearly the need involved. However, the flip side of such experiences is the need, also beginning early, to set appropriate limits for the child and stick to them. When these important principles are maintained through childhood, it then becomes easier to manage conflicts when the challenges of puberty arise in the teenage years.

Another important learning experience for children lies in their use of money. This begins in the common practice of giving children an allowance, and then monitoring the use of it. Additional income may come from a paper route or from babysitting. Again, the use of money should be monitored, and any developing faults may be pointed out as a learning experience. However, a word of caution here is needed! The very best guidance for children in the proper use of money is the example set by their parents. If parents are conservative in their use of money, especially in the use of credit cards, it is unlikely that the children will fall into the credit card trap. I have seen young people come to marriage with several thousand dollars in credit card balances. More and more, this seems to be an expected way of living in our world.

The art of communication and the use of money both refer to the reality of loving our children unconditionally. This requires that we love

---

them even when they are smart-mouthed and disrespectful. However, we must not fall into the permissive trap. Part of loving our child lies in the need to set appropriate limits and to model appropriate conduct. Much of the counseling that I have done with teens seems to indicate a problem at this very point. From my perspective, I realized that the parents really did love their child, but it was not expressed in a manner that was understood and accepted by the son or daughter.

Another factor that parents need to keep in mind is that in the teen and preteen years, the acceptance and approval of their peer group are more important to the child than the approval of their parents. As a result, the prevailing attitudes of the child tend to reflect the attitudes of the peer group. Despite this reality, it is imperative that the parents ignore this truth and KEEP ON TALKING! While children seem to ignore the advice of parents, they DO hear, and often in emergency situations, that advice rises up to save them. In view of this, it is both the consistent and persistent guidance of parents that makes the ultimate impression. If parents fail in this responsibility, the teens will adopt the values and morals of the peer group, rather than the mature guidance of their parents.

One of the hazards that I have observed in this context is the unconscious tendency of parents to relive some unrealized aspect of their childhood through a son or daughter. I recall an experience in which a man had only one son. The father had been a star lacrosse player, both in high school and college. His desire that his son follow in his footsteps is understandable, but the son did not like lacrosse and was not good at it. The father coerced the son into playing lacrosse in high school, but he never excelled in it. When he went to college, at the same school his father attended, the father insisted that he go out for lacrosse. At this point, the son refused, and his father was furious.

The father's angry insistence resulted in a serious breach in their relationship and also created marital stress because the mother understood the feelings of their son, and tried to protect him from his father's displeasure. I fear that the resulting explosion may lead to a permanent rift between father and son that may persist into adult life—all because the father tried to make his son over in his own image.

A similar problem occurred with a mother who had only one daughter. The mother's childhood had been rigidly puritanical. She was never allowed to wear makeup, and she was not allowed to begin to date until she was sixteen. After she married to escape the difficult environment in the home, her only daughter was born, and soon after the mother began to exhibit a curious ambivalence.

Verbally, and otherwise, the mother perpetuated the rigid, ultra-conservative morality of the home of origin, but her daughter grew up very pretty and also very precocious. By the age of ten the mother was buying expensive makeup and teaching her the art of using it. By middle school, her mother had her looking like a high school senior since her mother bought the latest fashions, sexy and revealing, and encouraged her daughter to wear them. This, as one may expect, made her an irresistible target for the boys, and the ambivalence she had previously been able to negotiate now became a mental and emotional catastrophe just waiting to happen. The young girl was faced with the classic double bind; which of her mother's directly opposite scripts should she follow? Since she was only fourteen, she made the obvious choice for a girl of her age. The conflict brought the onset of mental instability and a clouded future for a beautiful, young girl with exceptional potential. All because of her mother's unconscious effort to relive, through her daughter, the childhood and youth she had been denied in her own early life.

Every mother with more than one child (and some fathers) will insist that she loves each child exactly the same, but in her heart she knows that this is not exactly the truth. Subtle differences arise between mother and child, or father and child, often early in life, that have an unconscious but powerful influence in the developing relationship. Also, it is rather common for parents to act out their conflicts and differences through the children, thus unintentionally bringing the children into the emotional equation.

These patterns of interaction may result in alliances in the family that persist into adult life, often between mother and son, or father and daughter, but other configurations may also occur. Likewise, it is not unusual for these patterns to continue into the second generation, with the parents continuing the original alliance, and playing favorites with the grandchildren. Also, it seems clear that some alliances develop out of competition by the parents for the love and devotion of the child.

In the early years of marriage, in families of more than one child, sibling rivalry is a common concern. This occurs most frequently when the first child is four or five years of age when the second child is born.

Almost overnight, his/her secure place as the baby of the family is suddenly lost. The hostility felt by the firstborn may be openly expressed, but more commonly, it is covert, with deliberate acts like pinching or hitting the infant are hidden from the parents.

This is another area when wise and sensitive parenting becomes essential. One of the best strategies lies in creating a sense of anticipation in the older child throughout the pregnancy, by constant repetition and talking about the new baby as if he/she was already present. It is also helpful to have the older child to help paint the nursery, or any other preparation for the birth of the new brother or sister. Another surefire attraction is to have the doctor allow the older child to listen to the heartbeat of the unborn baby.

When the new baby arrives home from the hospital, allow the older child to hold the infant, and then in various appropriate ways to help care for the newcomer, such as holding a bottle in feeding or to entertain the little one with a rattle or a spinning mobile, or to replace a lost pacifier. Any such means will pay rich dividends through which the older child is given the opportunity to share in the ownership of the new baby, and also to share in the joy of having a new member of the family. Any such strategies will help to reduce the likelihood of sibling rivalry and to encourage the bonds of love between the children.

For young parents trying to cope with a new baby, and even more so when there are other children, one of the most common irritants and complaints is stress. Imagine a single mom with two small children, who must be up by five-thirty and begin to prepare for the day. She makes a hasty breakfast, takes one child to daycare, and drops the other off for preschool. She must be at work by eight, and often she is required to take a bus to get there.

In the afternoon, she leaves work at 5:00 and picks up both children. Then, at home, she must prepare dinner, and at the same time try to cope with two tired and cranky children. With dinner over, she must clean up the kitchen, shepherd the older child through homework, do some washing, and lay out clothing for the next day. She falls in bed exhausted at 11:00 p.m., and the only reward she sees is the need to repeat the same schedule the next day, and the next, and the next. Then throw in a sick child, with much loss of sleep, and a visit to the doctor for which she has neither the money nor the time. The older child must go to soccer, Cub Scouts, or gymnastics. Then, in her spare time, there is an urgent meeting with the P.T.A. You get the picture. Such stress taxes the weary body and boggles a mind operating constantly on overload.

Any discussion of parenting must include stepfamilies, for, in most of these merged families, parenting takes on a whole new meaning. I recall a case in family counseling in which a young mother was divorced and left to care for two daughters alone, with one daughter age two, and the other age six. For eight years, she carried on the heavy burden alone, seeing her valiant struggle as a needed sacrifice for her daughters. Then, she met a man, and in the course of time, she fell in love.

At first, indeed, for several months, there was excitement and enjoyment, with the girls finding delight in having a father figure who was around two or three nights a week. He occasionally took the family out to dinner or to the movies. The girls did not object when the mother brought in a trusted friend to stay with them while the mother enjoyed an infrequent night out. As their romance matured toward marriage and the boyfriend began to spend more time in the home, the attitude of the girls began a gradual change. They realized that the emotional capital of their mother was no longer lavished upon them alone, as in the past, since her love and attention were now divided. In response to these developments, the irritation and resentment of the girls became more apparent.

After the excitement of the wedding, in which the wise mother gave the girls some prominent participation, the now stepfather moved in and the honeymoon euphoria faded rapidly; in the gathering storm, the wheels began to come off the wagon. The daughters found endless things to gripe about and the mother found it difficult to understand the abrupt change in their behaviors.

The family situation was even more difficult for the stepfather, for the resentment of the girls spilled over and began to cloud the relationship between him and their mother. Whatever he did to try to pour oil on the troubled waters was usually misinterpreted, either by the mother or the daughters. If he dared to get involved in the inevitable family squabbles, or if he tried to support the efforts of the mother to discipline the girls, then he became the wicked stepfather, with all three of the females allied against him, charging him with trying to run their lives. On the other hand, if he tried to play it safe and remain neutral in these concerns of the family, then he was accused of not caring. It was a classic double bind; whatever he did was certain to be wrong.

My intervention in this rather typical case began through counseling with the girls, and in the course of time, I was able to help them to realize that they not only had the love and caring of their mother, but of the stepfather as well. Next, in working with the mother and her husband, I pointed out to them that their anger and frustration were self-defeating, and their best course of action would be found in building on the strengths they had in the family system, and through concentration on these positive factors.

I stressed the fact that the girls needed to be reassured that they were loved unconditionally, and to express their love in all of their interactions with them. Then I encouraged both girls to show their real affection for this new man in their lives through a hug and a kiss as they prepared for bed. The final exercise was to encourage both girls to talk about their feelings and for the adults to model frank and open communication and understanding in all of their problems. As understanding and trust deepened, this stepfamily became a real family, in the best sense of the term.

As we have indicated earlier, parenting in merged families requires special resources. Parenting skills will be tested on a daily basis since several personalities are involved in the dynamic interaction. Let me say here, without question, the most critical issue involved here is the relationship between the parents. If that relationship is secure, and they present a united front in working with the children, then the problems can always be worked out. However, there must always be complete love and trust. Any conflicts or differences must be settled privately, apart from the children. That love and trust modeled by the parents will be noted, and eventually each member of the family will practice it. However, the love of the parents must be expressed both by precept and example, in both word and deed. The next great principle in managing the stresses in a merged family is the art of communication. If every source of friction is fully explored and resolved, such stresses will be reduced to the minimum.

One startling result of the explosion of stepfamilies and divorces is a relatively new phenomenon in the number of young parents who are emotionally, mentally, or economically incapable of responsible parenting. In the vast majority of such cases, the grandparents must assume the heavy burden of taking young children into their home and raising a second family, often on a retired income. The emotional toll on these older persons has never been adequately explored, and surely, their contribution and sacrifice have never been fully appreciated in our social order.

From all of the above, it is clear that the family today is faced with serious challenges. Some are economic, but many are relational, particularly in various configurations of merged families. When marital relationships are so strained that a divorce seems to be the only solution, what happens in the lives of children? Who is most at fault seems to make little difference. Whatever the legal or social arrangements, these estranged parents are forced to interact with each other on a regular basis until the youngest child of the union is eighteen or older. Again, what are the emotional effects on the children? In many cases, it seems that they are the forgotten, or neglected, factor in the human equation.

Because of the emotional investments often involved in these unfortunate situations, the acrimony between the former spouses is not the only problem. As a result of real or imagined insults, the new spouse is often drawn into the fray as well. I had a recent case in which the relationship between the former wife and the new wife was so heated that when the father went to pick up the child for the weekend, he refused to take the new wife along because when he did, there was always an explosion. Add to this the resentment of the new wife, who must remain at home alone while the father makes the long trek at regular intervals to pick up the child for the weekend. Thoughtful people will wonder what effect this volatile mix must have on the emotional development of the child.

Whatever the sources of irritation or stress between divorced parents, the most important factor, that must be kept uppermost in the mind of both, is the well-being of the child or children involved. The relationship between these two parents is the source and the basis of their emotional security. The damage through the divorce is done, but the emotional trauma can be considerably reduced if both parents maintain a united front for the sake of the children, and out of their mutual love for them. One of the ways in which this united front may be damaged is through direct or indirect criticism of the absent parent. Any such reference should always be positive and affirming.

CHAPTER SIX:

The Launching Pad

It is perhaps only the first of our disappointments when we realize that the leaving home process does not begin at eighteen or twenty when the young adult goes off to work or to college, but rather when we watch our son or daughter go bravely down the walk, and climb up the steps of the school bus at the age of six. There are others—the first prom, when the daughter dons an adult-looking gown and the date for the evening appears in a tux and brings flowers. Then there is the first job at McDonald's, with the son or daughter going out at odd hours to work a split shift.

Another milestone is reached with graduation from high school at eighteen. At this point, the ambivalent feelings we have experienced before now take center stage. When you see your teenager walk across the platform wearing the cap and gown, and clutching the precious diploma, with numb sense of shock, you realize that you are standing in the door of tomorrow, between a yesterday you can never reclaim, and a tomorrow that belongs, no longer to you, but to him or her.

The same scene is repeated when your young adult goes off to college, to return only on semester breaks or special occasions. This experience leaves you with a hollow sound of emptiness echoing through the house. Or worse, when the son or daughter takes up residence with a new spouse, or leaves to take a new job, sometimes on the other side of the Atlantic. These separations come with a sense of finality that the occasional trips back home never quite seem to alleviate.

One such mother attended her daughter's wedding in Europe, with no weeks of preparation, no elaborate wedding, and with only the groom's parents in attendance. The adjustment was so difficult and wrenching that the daughter's room remained untouched for more than a year. This is a scenario with a hundred different details, yet each requires an emotional adjustment, especially for a mother, which may take months, or even years, to work through.

For many people today, however, it is not like this at all. Many parents today are wondering IF their young adult children will leave home, not WHEN. Traditionally, most young persons left home by age eighteen or twenty, either through marriage or needed changes brought about by school, work, or a career. For many years young adults longed for two things—separation from parents and freedom for independent living. The former is still sought eagerly, but the independence? That is another matter entirely. These changes have been years in transition, but the change has been progressive over the past quarter century.

In part, the explanations for these changes have been both cultural and sociological. The children of the depression grew up in a time of severe economic distress. Mere survival was a challenge, and unnecessary luxuries were non-existent. These children grew up and entered adult life in the growing affluence of the post-war years. Most of us have heard the common expression many times, "I will not allow my children to be deprived as we were." As a result, the pendulum has swung to the other extreme, and these post-war children were reared in a very permissive and indulgent environment. Because of these fortunate conditions, as someone has expressed it, "They are now high maintenance people." They have been conditioned to expect the best.

All of us have observed the result of this mind-set. Generally, these young adults marry later, simply because conditions are so comfortable at home. With a lifetime of relative privilege, they expect to begin their marriage at the same level of affluence as their parents, who have been saving and accumulating for thirty years or longer. In many cases, the only way they can maintain their accustomed lifestyle is through living beyond their means. This possibility has been provided for and encouraged by banks and other financial institutions, and as well, often by the example of their parents, and surely by the lifestyle of their peers, for whom the credit card is a fact of life.

Unfortunately, in most cases, no one has helped them to understand the facts of economic life. They are borrowing the extra money required at twenty percent interest, which compounds astronomically, and only a Bill Gates or Donald Trump could afford that. What happens next, as the wheels begin to come off the wagon? All too often, the financial stress is added to the other conflicts in their marriage, and they separate, with one or both "going home to mother."

We should note it is not only economic pressure alone that makes their life untenable. Because of the nature of their upbringing, many of these young adults do not possess the resources of character they need to live independently. I heard recently of a young woman who was returning to the home of her parents for the third time, this time with two small children. The extent of this exploitation of aging parents is sometimes unbelievable, and often the returning son or daughter tends to dominate the family, and takes no responsibility for themselves or their offspring, expecting their parents to take care of them as they did when they were children. I recently had a call from a distraught mother who was desperate. She was a widow who had financed her only daughter through four years of college followed by a master's degree. The daughter was working, but she was so undisciplined in the management of her money that she was evicted from her apartment. The mother took her in, but the condominium was too small and the mother bought a house in order to have enough living space. Unfortunately, she soon discovered that it was impossible for them to live together, since the daughter thought that life revolved around her.

Seeing no other alternative, she allowed the daughter to move into her condominium, despite the fact that the rental was providing the mother with a substantial monthly income. The result of this move was predictable; in a few months, the ungrateful girl had trashed the condominium to the extent that it was no longer livable. Through my counsel, at long last, the mother was encouraged to "let go" in this impossible situation, and the daughter was forced to make it on her own.

This unfortunate situation is not an isolated incident. Statistics indicate that from one-fourth to one-third of young adults from eighteen to thirty are still living at home with their parents, although this may vary somewhat geographically. The problem has become so pervasive and common that sociologists have devised an acronym for it. They are called ILYAs, or "Incompletely Leaving Young Adults." Another apt term for these prodigal sons and daughters is "The Boomerang Generation." They go out, but all too often, they also come back. Parents who find themselves in this dilemma are faced with two difficult choices, either to take the young adult in, often with one or more children, or to provide necessary assistance in order for the son or daughter to live with some degree of independence. In many cases, the latter course is precluded by the level of financial support needed. Often, the young person moves back in with no prearranged agreement as to terms or conditions. "It's just until I can get back on my feet." If not addressed, this is an invitation to a semi-permanent arrangement.

It may be observed that this situation is also an invitation to abuse. With any set of parents who are faced with this problem, it is imperative that some boundaries be established. First, a time limit should be set that is clearly understood and agreed upon, whether one month, six months, or longer. Secondly, some ground rules should be set and agreed upon, whereby the young person moving in must assume certain personal responsibilities. If no rent is paid, then some commitment should be made to assist in living expenses. Also, some guidelines should be set up relative to daily needs in the home, such as help with cooking, cleaning, laundry, and the care of their own room or rooms, and other sharing of family needs. In this, the cogent advice of the poet, Robert Frost, has special significance, "Good fences make good neighbors."

In such boomerang cases, the prior training received in the home becomes critical, particularly the training in character and values that were established. If these lessons in living were modeled by the parents and practiced in the home, with the proper principles having been instilled, many of the behavioral problems sometimes seen will be avoided, and coexisting with adult children can be a positive experience.

There is a flip side to grown children leaving home, and that concerns the parent who will not or cannot, let go. In many of these cases, the emotional needs of the parent are the underlying problem. I recall one such case that I had the privilege to observe over a period of years. It was an only-child situation, and the only son's father had died at an early age. This emotional loss made the mother fiercely protective of her son. She never dated, had no further relations with men, and as a result, she had a very limited social life. Instead, she devoted all of her emotional capital to her son. She never allowed him to have other children over to play, or to visit in the homes of other boys.

As one might expect, this limited socialization created problems in the emotional development of the son. As he grew into the preteen and teen years and began to show an interest in girls, it appeared that the mother had Xray vision. Any mention of a girl's name brought on a tirade from the mother, and a vicious campaign of character assassination of the hapless victim. The ultimate result was that he was never permitted to go to youth programs or teen dances as a teenager, or to date, as he grew older. Any interest he expressed in activities outside the home was met by the charge that he didn't love his mother, or he was neglecting her. It is not surprising that he found it difficult to relate to people in social situations. The mother maintained her rigid control, and he became more and more isolated as her mental and physical condition declined and she demanded even more attention from him. After her death, he was severely handicapped emotionally, and this talented man, with so much potential, was confined to a largely reclusive life, unable to relate comfortably with people. All because of a neurotic and controlling mother who could not let him go.

I also had the opportunity to observe a similar situation, but with the opposite gender. The father in question was a prosperous farmer, who through astute financial management and the profitable sale of some of his acreage, branched out into real estate and development. Meanwhile, he had two daughters and four sons. Perhaps as a result of sheltering by the mother, the girls seemed to escape the most severe domination of the father, but it was a very different condition for the sons.

With the sons, the father was dictatorial, if not tyrannical. Literally from birth, he demanded instant obedience from the boys, and he exercised rigid control over their lives. While they were permitted to date, the father did not hesitate to use his veto power with any girl who failed to meet with his approval. His sons were not allowed to develop any personal discretion or judgment since their father made all of the daily decisions for them. All four eventually married and left home, but they, too, were severely handicapped, being totally dependent upon their father. As a result, they were incapable of managing their own lives in any practical way. I have been led to wonder what their lot in life may be when their father dies or becomes incapacitated. Like most of the controlling parents I have known, both male and female, it seems likely that his inner motivation was not merely to control for its own sake, but rather he felt that his judgment was better for them.

I saw a young woman in therapy over a period of two years who was the angriest person I have ever met. She was an only child, and in many respects, she was a paradox, for she came from a good family with all of the resources of moderately wealthy people. The father was a rather colorless personality who was just there, but seemingly made no contribution in his daughter's life. Her mother was a career businesswoman whose primary preoccupation was her business. She had the financial resources to buy for her daughter the latest fashions in clothing, and she spared no effort in training the little girl in the social graces, and in making sure that she attended all of the "right" social events with the best people.

In her personality type, however, the mother was aloof and unemotional. In her interactions with her only child, she was "too busy" to spend time with her except in what she felt was necessary training. In describing her relationship with her mother, the daughter told me that she could never remember her mother holding her, kissing her, or providing any level of comfort or emotional support. It was also interesting to me that it was not the mother who brought her into counseling, but the daughter, who recognized the fact that she had some serious emotional problems, at least in part, because she had difficulty in relating to other people.

In the course of therapy, she eventually began to see that it is not the things that happen to us through the sometimes strange twists of life, but rather how we react to these events, and our response to them. She was able to realize that there was some level of caring in her mother, but it was never expressed in a manner that was meaningful to her. While the mother now more clearly understands the deficits she created in her daughter, and there is a greater degree of awareness of the problems between mother and daughter, it seems most unlikely that there will be a real adult relationship between them. While the mother now has a more mature grasp of her lack of emotional support in her only daughter's life, there is now no way that she can go back in time and correct it. This case material illustrates the absolute truth that the only way one may have a real emotional interdependence with a son or daughter is to nurture that emotional interaction from the stages of infancy through childhood. It is too late to realize the need or the desire for such a relationship, and try to foster it later.

However, the past remains in the past, and it is possible that with growing maturity on the part of all concerned, and with the recognition that times and circumstances do change, there is always the possibility that even deep-seated anger and resentment may be overcome by understanding and forgiveness, and that past failures may be negated by love and concern expressed in the now. It seems so tragic that we may sometimes allow the past to cloud and shape the future as well.

In another case that illustrates the link between the separation process and our experiences in earlier life, a young man of twenty was referred to me by his mother. He was depressed and demonstrating serious problems with both anger and aggression. His family history was interesting. Both of his parents were professional people with advanced degrees. They had two children and both were boys. The older son was a typical firstborn, who was alert, intelligent like his parents, very serious and obedient, and eager to please. As you might expect, he was a favorite with his teachers and an excellent student.

The second lad was totally different; he seemed slower, and tended to be klutzy. He had an independent streak and tended to follow his own agenda. Although his parents had him tested, there was some concern on their part that he had some level of handicap. This issue was further complicated by the fact that he followed his bright and highly motivated brother through school. There was constant comparison, with some of his teachers making the exasperated comment, "Why can't you be like your brother?" While his parents never made such an obvious comparison, he always seemed to be in the shadow of his older brother.

In view of these experiences in his earlier life, it is uncertain whether he ever really made his best effort in school, or whether he concluded that it was just not worth the effort and simply gave up. He graduated from high school with barely passing grades, and there was no expectation that he could succeed in college, so this was never an option. All of these negative dynamics compounded, and together they seriously damaged his self-image. He floundered after leaving school and bounced around several entry-level jobs, never lasting more than a few weeks in any. Given his history, it is not surprising that he drifted into drinking, often to excess, and he was also experimenting with drugs. His mother brought him into therapy after some minor scrapes with the police. His anger level at that time had almost reached the point of explosion. Although he had never been caught, he was engaged in deliberate acts of serious vandalism, venting his anger by blowing out the windows of parked cars with a shotgun. In our first few sessions, he was guarded and suspicious, feeling that I was in league with his parents. My preliminary screening indicated that he was not handicapped, as his parents suspected. Instead, he was alert, at times bright, when he was motivated and challenged.

As his trust level grew, he became more open, particularly in his feelings toward his family. His pattern of drinking was reduced to the point that it was no longer a serious concern, and his experimentation with drugs ended. Within a year, his self-image had improved considerably. He was beginning to feel a sense of pride within himself and to look forward to a more promising future. This alteration in his attitude had a positive effect on his work performance. He was now able to keep a job and to attract the attention of his superiors, which earned him a raise.

He was a large, exceptionally handsome lad, with more potential than either his teachers or even his parents had recognized. With time on his hands that I suspected might become a problem, I encouraged him to enroll in a course in a community college, where he surprised everyone with his commitment and determination, as well as his above-average grade-point standing. By this time, he had won a newfound respect from his parents, who now realized that they had been part of his problems in their failure to see the possibilities in him and to encourage his growth. This case history indicates how easily parents may be led to unjustified conclusions, and how the erosion of self-image can occur through repeated negative influences.

The physical needs of growing children are the easy ones: food, clothing, shelter, and relative security. The emotional needs are more obscure, though not less important. All parents have gone through the changes of youth, but our memories fade with time. For teens, there are both inner and outer struggles, with conflicts between independence and dependence, between growing maturity and innate immaturity. Then there are the physical changes. For the boys, it is the awkward and gangly growth spurts, including a cracking voice. For girls, it is the secondary growth changes, with the onset of the menstrual cycle and breast development.

The response to these is often a sense of frustration and resentment over these inner conflicts, which they do not understand, and yet they cannot escape. Often youth in this age group will act out in order to get attention. Normal expressions and reactions of youth are reflected in their choice of music, the manner in which they dress (they seem to prefer looking like a fugitive from a flea market), and often strange hairstyles.

It sometimes appears that the more outrageous their appearance, the happier they are with it. However, these are normal reactions, and they are almost to be expected. There are also abnormal reactions, such as radical change in eating habits, changes in normal emotional reactions, and depression. Parents must be alert to any change from the normal, because these are ALWAYS a cry for help.

These warning signs may include bouts of depression, which are very foreign to the natural exuberance of youth, or panic attacks and eating disorders such as anorexia or bulimia. Also, any violent behavior is a danger signal, and parents must approach this with the realization that there is a reason for it. Any change in personality and any loss in school grades should be a cause for concern. Likewise, parents should be alert to any variation in a young person's reaction to their peer group, or to any evidence of withdrawal, anger, or any other unusual response to friends.

As noted previously, out of a desire for success for a son or daughter, parents may set them up for failure through expectations too high for them to attain. Throughout childhood, and particularly through the teen years, a dedicated effort must be made to develop a positive self-image. The flip side of this concern is to watch closely for any evidence of a poor self-image. It is helpful to note that body image is a critical part of the self-image for a teen, and any body stature that is beyond normal parameters, either too skinny or too much overweight, may subject a child to merciless teasing at a time when they are least able to cope with it.

The most commonly felt need among teens is the drive to fit in and to be an accepted member of their peer group. This makes them even more receptive (and vulnerable) to influences beyond the orbit of their parents. This can lead to unwise and unwelcome activities, and adults should be aware of the powerful attraction of M.T.V. in making alcohol, drugs, and premature sexual activity seem glamorous and irresistible to the youth culture. In this respect, parents may find it helpful to point out that freedom and responsibility are closely related, indeed they are opposite sides of the same coin, and the more responsible they prove themselves to be, the more freedom will be allowed to them. In dealing with these sensitive issues, parents must ALWAYS make a clear distinction between the person and the behavior.

CHAPTER SEVEN:

The Separation Process

It should surprise no one that the separation process does not begin in the late teens or the early twenties, but rather in the preteen years, from ten to twelve. The dynamics involved will vary in terms of gender, whether male or female, and the process is affected by the number of children, and whether an only child, or two or more. The age of the parents is also relevant, particularly the age of the mother. The age of parents going through these changes is usually from thirty-five to forty-five, with some variation. In general, the separation process involves the same gender parent more directly. Girls must rebel against their mothers, while boys must rebel against their fathers. It is at this point that the quality of parenting becomes critical. If either parent is insecure, this tends to complicate the experience. This may occur through the need by the parent to keep the child dependent and emotionally immature, but the opposite may also come about, where the parent most involved claims dependence on the young adult. "You can't leave me yet, because I need you." It is not unusual to find a situation of mutual dependence, in which each needs the other to function comfortably.

The separation begins in the need of the young adult for independence, and one of the more critical factors here is the need to establish emotional independence. Some parents may try to hold on to a grown child through economic dependence, although this is secondary. To express it in another way, the young adult must find the strength to leave emotionally before he can leave physically. It is at this point that the quality of parenting through the childhood and teen years becomes most apparent.

If the same-sex parent is emotionally mature, the dynamics of the separation process should not leave residual problems in the relationship in the years to come. Also, if the opposite gender bonding has been close, the father is able to support the daughter in her struggle to be free from her mother, and conversely, a close relationship with the mother provides the emotional security needed by the son in seeking independence from his father. In each case, there is a declaration of independence, making it possible and necessary for the young adult to find himself, or herself, in the grown-up world.

It must be emphasized that this separation from the ties of home is not an event, but an evolving experience that works out over time, with the young person constantly testing and expanding the boundaries of freedom. One of the difficult factors here is that, at least with the first child leaving home, neither the child nor the parents clearly understand what is happening, largely because of the emotional overtones involved. In counseling with youth struggling with this experience, I have often had the same question to be asked, "Why am I doing this?" The perplexity of the parent is equally apparent. Again, one of the hard lessons, that parents must somehow teach their children seeking freedom, is that freedom and responsibility are opposite sides of the same coin.

As we leave the childhood scene through the process of separation, two observations need to be made. The first is that the family is an operating system, and anything that affects one member will ultimately touch the whole family. The family may be compared to a group of passengers traveling on a bus. They may be diverse, but they are all enclosed in the same vehicle. Anything that happens on the bus will affect every passenger. Conversely, anything that occurs with one passenger will touch everyone aboard in some significant way also. Anything that touches one family member will eventually involve the whole family system.

Another reality familiar to anyone studying the family is the process of scapegoating, and while it is familiar, it is not well understood by many parents. It often seems to be arbitrary or indiscriminate in the member of the family elected for this dubious distinction, but in many families with more than one child, one of the children becomes "it." That person is assumed to be responsible, either directly or indirectly, for all of the ills that beset the family system. From the outside, it may be seen as unfair and discriminating, but the reality of the process is beyond question. Any new family will be well advised to be vigilant as the family develops, and thus to prevent this damaging process from infecting their family. With the separation process now concluded, we may turn our attention to the next stage in the life of the family—the relationship of parents with their adult children.

CHAPTER EIGHT:

Relationships With Adult Children

To the couple involved in the separation process, and particularly so when one or more children remained in the home until the mid-twenties, there has been some speculation and anticipation as to how it may feel, especially from the perspective of the mother, when there is "one less egg to fry," one-third less laundry to do each week, and another room available for some long-delayed purpose. The unspoken question then becomes, "What happens next?" For most couples at the end of the empty nest, there is a sense of freedom from long disciplines and priorities that no longer exist. There is freedom to do things long deferred, and sometimes for the mother, there is the opportunity to go back to school and study French or Spanish, or even to take a part-time job, and for both, there is the possibility to pursue common interests, such as travel or collecting antiques.

The unexpected reality for both husband and wife is that the empty nest signals a return to the primary relationship they established at their wedding forty years ago. For some, it comes with the recognition that their attention has been centered on the children for such a long time that their relationship has been subtly altered, without either of them being conscious of the change. This new reality offers the possibility for their life together to take on a new dimension, almost like another beginning.

"The Empty Nest Syndrome." This rather pompous title suggests a comprehensive clinical picture whose nature is clearly understood, with every facet having been carefully explored and evaluated. However, any couple that has survived the experience will tell you that this is not exactly true. While every older couple dreams of the day when the last child leaves for college, or leaves home for work, it always comes with a heavy heart, for the parents are a generation older; they understand that the life in the home will never be the same again. The mother remembers when the six-year-old walked bravely down the walk to get on the school bus for the first time, without even looking back, and any mother willing to talk about it will admit that they spent most of that day in tears.

What does it mean when the youngest daughter marries and moves out of the home at twenty-two? It signals the end of a critical phase in marriage and family life. A house that was filled with laughter and music seems strangely still. Most couples who share this experience do not really understand its meaning, except in retrospect, because far more is taking place than the last child leaving home. For most families, the empty nest occurs at a crucial time in the life cycle for both men and women, in age usually from forty-five to fifty, or above.

For both, there is the awareness of the loss of youth, not yet old, but definitely no longer young. In some studies, this era is often referred to as "The Foolish Forties." The apparent key as to how any individual weathers this storm lies in one's self-image. People, who are realistic, secure, and satisfied with their roles in life, sail serenely through this period with little sense of problem or concern. For those who are insecure and anxious about the mounting years, forty is a dreaded milestone on the road of life.

For men in this age bracket, most realize that they are at or near the top of the ladder, and that they have already achieved most of the success that is probable for them. This is the period in life when they begin to see younger men with less experience promoted before them, and they sense an almost imperceptible drift downward. Most men in their forties are conscious of some loss of youthful vigor and energy, with some degree of loss in athletic ability. The Orioles' superstar, the "Iron Man," Cal Ripken, is a classic example. His long career as an Oriole has been an inspiration to many young men, particularly his Iron Man record of 2,632 consecutive games played. This record is not likely to be broken soon, if ever. Yet, Cal was secure enough in what he had accomplished, that he was able to leave the game he loved so much with exceptional grace and without any serious injuries.

This era is the age at which some men divorce the girl of their youth and marry a woman ten or fifteen years younger. Or there is the man of fifty, who on the spur of the moment goes out and buys a Corvette, or a big Harley-Davidson, or he may become involved with a young woman at the office, all in a futile effort to turn back the fleeting pages of time. This is also the time when a man may incur a heart attack, again in an effort to prove that he can still compete with younger men.

This age is perhaps more difficult for women, for whom the age of forty often creates a second identity crisis. This is particularly true for the woman with three or four children who has had the privilege of staying at home with the children. In her case, the major purpose in her life has been that of a mother. Then when the last child leaves home, she is suddenly faced with a harsh reality: "If I am not a mother, who am I?" If she has been a career woman, then this is the age when the women at the office throw a big party, "Lordy, Lordy, look who's forty!" There seems to be a considerable amount of malevolent glee that another woman must join the over-forty club. At this point, the woman who is insecure begins to notice the appearance of wrinkles. The size eight dress has become a ten or twelve, because her metabolism has slowed down, and she begins to put on some unwanted pounds. She tends to look at the vibrant and sexy young woman of twenty-five, and she not only feels the loss of youth, but she also fears the loss of sexuality. Not surprisingly, the forties is the era when some women long to take one more fling at life, then after a divorce, they date younger men, and eventually marry "a hunk," who is fifteen or twenty years younger than herself. These June and September marriages seldom last.

I believe that mothers have a more difficult time in dealing with the empty nest than most fathers, because they have normally invested more of their emotional capital with their children, and for them, the empty room does not seem like a transition, but a permanent loss. Considering all of the above, and looking back over forty years of work with families, the derogatory term, "The foolish forties," often proves itself to be true.

However, as noted previously, both men and women who are secure within themselves and who accept a realistic view of aging, manage the concerns of the empty nest and the years following with grace and confidence. Among other things, these challenges represent a real test of the strength and stability of a marriage. The man who thinks his wife is beautiful at twenty-five will also think that she is beautiful at fifty. It is in that sense of love and trust, that secure feeling of belonging, that each finds the strength, not only to navigate these times of troubled waters, but to look forward to the coming years together with faith and anticipation.

The last young adult leaving home is a reminder that first, before they had children, they were only a couple, and now they are back to that primary relationship, and they are a couple again. Often I hear the comment, "They are so lucky that they have such a wonderful life together." In the world of today, such marriages may be more rare than they should be, but I suspect that luck is seldom a factor. Good marriages do not "just happen," rather it requires two people in love who are constantly adapting and seeking to improve the quality of their life together.

What happens when this hoped for and expected event does not follow? Often, the end result is that the young adult does not possess the maturity and character he needs to cope with the outside world that seems difficult and demanding, and it presents a challenge that he is not yet ready to tackle. As noted previously, it is not uncommon for middle-aged parents to have one or more adult children living at home, despite being thirty years of age. In many cases, it is perhaps immaturity or even just plain laziness, but often the problem is sheer economics.

Thirty years ago, it was possible for a young couple to marry and move out on their own on one entry-level salary. This is not possible today. Both must work and at entry-level incomes, there will be few luxuries beyond the necessities of food and rent. Data recently released indicates that rental costs in Maryland are the fourth highest in the nation. Many college graduates discover that the competition in the job market is so severe today that they must have a master's degree in order to land a job. In many cases, this will assure them of two more years at home with their parents paying most, if not all, of the bills. A frustrated parent probably wrote the following: "CHILDREN! ARE YOU TIRED OF BEING HARRASSED BY YOUR STUPID PARENTS? ACT NOW! MOVE OUT! GET A JOB, PAY YOUR OWN BILLS, WHILE YOU STILL KNOW EVERYTHING."

Often today, beyond the underlying economic challenge, there is a very real fear for many young adults in trying to cope with the outer world alone. The major problems may be immaturity and insecurity. In the permissive and affluent age in which most of these young adults were reared, moving out would demand a radical loss in their standard of living that many are not willing to accept. Similarly, others were not given the progressive responsibility in their growing-up years that would prepare them for successfully coping with the demands of adult life. A recent article in the *Baltimore Sun* by Eileen Ambrose examines the dilemma posed by Boomerang young adults. "Across the country, more and more parents are finding their young adult children returning home to live for months or even years, when they had expected them to be deep in their own lives. The latest census figures show that 56% of men and 43% of women ages 18 to 24 live with one or both parents. These so-called "Boomerang Kids" appear on their doorsteps for reasons that include a lack-luster job market, health problems, divorce, or the realization that they can't afford the life-style that their parents offer. Young adults who come home frequently expect to pick up where they left off, living rent-free in their old room, with mom and dad footing the bills, experts say . . . Many such children arrive deep in debt, and some parents feel obligated to bail them out."

It is not unusual in such cases for the parents to pay the car insurance for son or daughter, with some providing a cash allowance monthly, sometimes generous, and I have known cases in which parents paid child support for a son who had boomeranged back home. Many such parents who welcome a son or daughter back home acknowledge that they would never have dreamed of doing such a thing when they were young.

What has transpired, socially and culturally, to allow such things to happen? There is the deep suspicion that the process begins in the over-indulgence of these young adults when they were children. They have grown up surrounded by the best, and as a result, they are now high maintenance people, with the feeling developed over the years that they are entitled to such a comfortable and privileged lifestyle. I recall one situation in which an adult son, an only child, continued to shamelessly exploit a doting mother until her death.

Circumstances may vary from one situation to another, but in consideration of the high percentage of these boomerang young adults today, there must certainly be some common denominators. To mention a single obvious problem, apparent in many of these cases, one may note the apparent lack of responsibility, and then ask, how does such a serious personality flaw develop? And why is it so apparent now? Surely, the cultural shift of the population from an agrarian setting to an urban or suburban lifestyle is a factor.

All country children grow up with progressive levels of responsibility, with daily assigned chores, beginning in childhood. Compare that with the current condition where children are expected to do little or nothing, complaining bitterly if they are asked to wash the dishes, or occasionally mow the lawn, or even if they are asked to clean up their room. Then these young teens who have never been responsible for anything graduate from high school. We march them across the stage in academic gowns and square hats, give them their diploma with a handshake, and say to them symbolically if not actually, "You are now a man or a woman." How unrealistic can we really be?

Then we expect them to move confidently into college, and after four years of undergraduate work, and perhaps two or three more years of graduate school, to enter a lucrative career and settle down to a successful life in the community. However, given our current cultural conditions, should we really be surprised that it fails to happen in a tragically high percentage of cases? I believe that responsible living begins with parents who consistently model these positive traits of character, and then begin molding this virtue in their children, from early childhood up through the teen years. Then they are trained to be independent, to accept responsibility for the choices they make, and to take just pride in their accomplishments.

Some young adults today simply do not possess the qualities of character demanded for independent living. Some are lazy, self-centered, and unwilling to step out into the adult world with the needed level of self-confidence. One of these pampered misfits with a master's degree expressed it so eloquently: "The nine-to-five world of work is a drag. It doesn't interest me." Some further indication that something rather drastic has happened to the work ethic and the pioneering spirit in the soul of the nation may be seen in this observation: Eighty years ago my father and mother were married at sixteen, and both were more mature and responsible than many young adults today at thirty.

Whatever the underlying problems may be, and however complex, there has been a large increase in the number of young adults who feel that the only solution in their situation lies in returning to the safe haven of their parents' home. This phenomenon has become so common that they are often referred to as the "Boomerang Generation." They go out, but all too often, they also return. In fairness to males, it should be noted that it is more often the daughter who finds it necessary to "Go back home to mother."

In any case, it poses a "catch-22" for parents. Either they must take the son or daughter in, with whatever dislocation this may require for them, or to make sometimes substantial financial sacrifices to provide an alternative solution. The more common solution is the former, which often necessitates physical changes in the home, since the daughter may bring one or more children with her. Yet, most parents faced with this problem will tell you that the physical adjustments are the least difficult. It is the emotional and relational aspects that create the most serious concerns.

In most cases, and particularly where there are children involved, the mother is expected to provide free child care when the mother is working, and also any babysitting for the daughter's dating or other social engagements. In such cases of boomerang returns, a fact of life should be recalled. Parents can be exploited by adult children only if they allow it to happen. Another adage also applies, "Can the leopard change its spots?" The emphatic answer is "NO!" A son or daughter who has been irresponsible will continue to follow the same careless pattern unless there is some significant intervention, but there is no important reason why the parents should allow themselves to be victimized through the pattern of failure by an adult son or daughter.

From an economic perspective, one of the most damaging factors in the manipulation of parents by an adult child is continued financial dependence. I have seen case after case in which an irresponsible offspring will remain dependent upon a parent, or parents, who continually bail them out when they need money, and they feel no regret or even concern until the money runs out. The classic case in literature is the story of the Prodigal Son, in the New Testament. When his inheritance had been squandered and he found himself starving, what was his first reaction? "I will go back home to my father"—and in virtually all such cases, they are assured of a sympathetic and caring response.

The critical question for parents faced with this dilemma is the need to carefully and prayerfully ponder whether the aid requested will really help the young adult, or whether it will merely perpetuate financially irresponsible patterns. I have helped parents to raise the question with a son or daughter as to when these so-called loans actually become gifts, with no realistic hope that they will ever be repaid. The answer to this question may lead to some honest soul-searching by the parents, and the response may lead to a healthy, if painful, change in the spending habits of the son or daughter, and possible progress toward financial independence.

A recent experience is a good example of the dynamics often involved in the boomerang scenario. An elderly couple was more than twenty-five years past the empty nest with their children, and both are now past eighty years of age. Their oldest son had married and left home thirty years previously. His marriage had been rocky from the start, but they had made a sincere effort to work out their differences.

The son had been working for the same company for thirty years, but in the downturn in the economy over the past two years, there were layoffs, and the son lost his job. Despite distributing his resume widely, and strenuous efforts to find work, at sixty he was unable to find work in his field of expertise. The unemployment compensation soon ran out, and while his wife was working, her income could not cover all of the basic expenses. Their only recourse was the credit card, hoping and expecting that something would work out for them.

However, the labor market is difficult, at best, and he was unable to find employment. The bills piled up, and the aggravating phone calls from collectors became a daily nuisance. These economic woes compounded other conditions in their relationship, and the marital stress reached the boiling point. In desperation, the son left home, rented a small car, and drove until it ran out of gas. With no money and no other resource available, he called his aging parents, who turned in the rental car and brought him to their home. Now, with thanks to his parents, he had a roof over his head, he had some respite from the marital strife, and the opportunity to seek employment in another geographical area, and the possibility to find some semblance of control in his life, and to invest some hope in his future.

The measure of compassion and caring displayed by the parents is commendable, and, I suspect, is common to most parents. However, we cannot ignore the cost to them in this process. Here we have two elderly people who have earned these years of peace and freedom from stress, but because of their caring, they are now subject to all of the stresses and crises in the life of their son. This includes what may become a long drawn-out marital confrontation between the son and his wife, with a good possibility that it will end in a divorce. The boundaries between his life and their lives have been broken down, and now, through no fault of their own except in caring for their son, the problems in his life have become unwelcome complications in their lives as well.

This painful vignette is as modern as the headline in today's newspaper, and yet, it is as old as Adam and Eve standing over the body of their son, Abel, and looking into the scowling face of their first son, Cain, who had murdered him. It is the pain of being a parent, and no parent has been completely free from it. Yet, these tragedies of life cannot compare with the joy of looking down into a newborn infant's face, of watching his first wobbly step, the pride we feel in the graduation of a son or daughter from college, to feel the mixture of love and loss in a wedding, or to hold a grandchild in your arms. This is life giving birth unto itself, and it is priceless.

There is yet another source of anxiety in this age group, and while it is not new, it is occurring with greater frequency as a result of the destructive forces affecting the family today. Only one generation ago, this phenomenon was rare, but today, it is astonishing to discover the frequency in which grandparents are being forced by dire circumstances to assume full responsibility for rearing grandchildren. In most cases, it is brought about through the incompetence of adult children trying to be parents, a failure often brought about by the ravages of alcohol or drugs. While the causation may vary from one case to another, the end result is that two older adults, who have lived through the demands of raising their own family, must now in middle age accept the emotional and financial burdens of bringing a second family to maturity. In the great majority of instances, they are bringing into the lives of these children a level of security they have never known.

Thus far, we have looked at the headaches and the heartaches imposed upon this forty—to sixty-year age group by their children and grandchildren, but this is only half of the story, for this age group is also called the "Sandwich Generation." They are caught between the needs of their adult children and grandchildren, and the needs of aging parents. Unlike the boomerang problem, the needs of aging parents are progressive. They tend to become more complex and demanding with the passing of the years. Again, these concerns will vary from one family to another, but there is no way to escape the inevitable passage of time. While this generation of the aging has inherited some of the rugged independence of their parents, and they have also benefited from improved nutrition and health care, the decades of the seventies and eighties bring to all the progressive effects of aging.

We have all heard the familiar litany of the newsprint getting smaller, and the stairs growing steeper. Another one of the signs of aging is that all of the names in your little black book end in M.D. Perhaps Erma Bombeck said it best, "At our age, everything hurts, and anything that doesn't hurt, doesn't work!" However well our parents may have managed in earlier years, the time comes when they can no longer drive, and in many cases, there is no public transportation available, and someone must drive them to medical and dental appointments, to the drug store for prescriptions, to the supermarket for groceries, and a hundred other needs too numerous to mention.

There are examples in which a couple has three or four children who live near enough to share in the common burdens of caring for aging parents, but these are relatively rare. The common refrain is, "I'm too busy," or "I live too far away," but the reality is that one son or daughter becomes the responsible one, who assumes the lion's share of the progressive responsibilities in the care of elderly parents. The others sit on the sidelines waiting for the opportunity to collect their equal share in the last surviving mate's estate.

In some fortunate circumstances, one spouse is well enough and strong enough to care for an aging mate until the end, or nearly so, but this is unusual. In some cultures, such as the Amish, or Pennsylvania Dutch, there is a strong family tradition of caring for the elderly. Many of their homes have a "Grandmother's House," either joining or a part of the main house, where aging parents are cared for until they die. Although they are old and perhaps handicapped, they continue to share in household chores as long as they are able to do so. However, this tradition is largely local, and relatively uncommon, except among the above culture.

Here again, as in the myriad of problems with adult children, the needs of aging parents are often urgent, and they may continue for years. When my father-in-law retired, he and my mother-in-law moved from the east coast to California (where some members of the family were located). For fifteen years, my wife felt obligated to make the long trip by air for each family crisis. Although there were other family members, she was the responsible one. In another situation, an aged father died, and his widow continued to live alone in the family home. She had never learned to drive and her daughter-in-law made regular jaunts of eighty-five miles each way, once or twice a week, to take her to appointments with a doctor or dentist, or to the pharmacy for a prescription, to the supermarket for groceries, or other personal needs.

In some cases, these weekly or daily needs may be compounded by special conditions such as Alzheimer's disease or other forms of dementia, often requiring a considerable investment of time and energy. Other critical health problems, such as advanced cases of cancer, or stroke victims, impose great stress on family members, and in most situations where it is possible, the aging father or mother would prefer to die at home, surrounded by the love and special care given by the family. In such cases, the hospice care program is a treasured resource, and home care by visiting nurses or other home care professionals often provide a much-needed respite for over-stressed family members. Even such a simple resource as a hospital bed can greatly simplify caring for an ill parent.

The Old Testament Book of Ecclesiastes reminds us, "To everything there is a season, and a time for every purpose under heaven." Also, "He has made everything beautiful in its time." In these stages of life, each period has its special blessings and its challenges, but for the Sandwich Generation, caught between the many problems of the Boomerang Generation, on the one side, and the inevitable demands of aging parents on the other, some level of burnout is understandable. As someone has observed, "It is hard to keep one's mind on draining the swamp when you are up to your neck in alligators."

CHAPTER NINE:

Retirement

The wisdom of the ages tells us that this, too, will pass, and in our journey through the life cycle, the next phase in the intervening years is the preparation for retirement. The term "preparation" is well chosen, for retirement is not an event, but a process, and the unwary person who does not understand the process, or neglects it, is in for some unpleasant surprises.

Fortunately, we live in a day in which there has been much concern about the quality of life. We have the best medical care in our history, and the Baby Boomers among us have a collective desire to live forever. As a result of these dynamics, there has been a virtual explosion of self-help studies to keep us emotionally balanced and relatively content. The nutrition experts keep our minds focused on a healthy diet, and the oriental influences, to which we have become so enamored, have given us everything from acupuncture to yoga, and with this, a thousand nutritional supplements, from the brain power in ginkgo biloba to the many restorative qualities of ginseng. At the same time, there has been an explosive increase of interest in physical conditioning. The fitness gurus beset us daily with the urgent need for flat abs, and we spend hours each week in a variety of regimens in our mostly futile efforts to look like Arnold Schwarzenegger. A steady diet of weight-loss programs promise to make us look like models, yet at the same time, they are reminding us that we are out of shape and overweight.

As a result of these dynamic influences and a plethora of physical resources, this group of persons approaching retirement is probably more fit than any previous generation in our history. The expected life span for both men and women has increased significantly, and these positive developments have not only added years to our lives, they have also added life to our years. While we are in the midst of an economic slump or depression, the past years since World War II have been largely prosperous, and the standard of living for most people has risen accordingly.

In the pre-retirement years today, you will find people traveling more, internationally as well as domestically. It is not unusual for people of modest means today to have a summer place on the ocean or a cabin in the mountains. Pursuits such as golf, once the province of the wealthy, are much more available to working class people, which serves to explain the crowded golf courses around metropolitan areas.

In an earlier day, a good pension was the expected norm for corporate workers, but in the present economic climate, this is no longer true for many. The meltdown in the tech areas and the vicious three-year bear market have taken a severe toll for many workers. In this same period, the IRAs and the 401K plans generally have lost from one-third to one-half of their former value. This catastrophic event has forced many workers, who had planned to retire early at sixty-two or sixty-five, to reconsider and now they must continue working. When they do retire, they will not be able to maintain the standard of living that they had expected to enjoy under earlier and more favorable conditions.

Under the best of circumstances, retirement is another life experience, and most writers in the field suggest a minimum of five years in planning to precede it. To move overnight, from a regimen of demanding activity to an experience of doing nothing, will bring a high level of stress on a person in all levels of one's being—physical, mental, and emotional, and it is essential that careful preparation must be integrated into the process.

For most persons approaching retirement, the place to begin is the economics. To go from a full salary to income from Social Security and perhaps a small pension, will usually involve a substantial reduction in income, which also dictates a change in lifestyle. Such a radical adjustment requires thought and anticipation, and in most cases, this will require years of careful planning in advance.

For many employees in recent years, retirement funding through an IRA, 401K, Keogh, or some similar savings plan, they have laid aside substantial assets to offset the loss of salary upon retirement. One of the best features of these retirement programs is that they are tax-deferred until the funds are withdrawn after retirement, when the reduced income results in a lower tax bracket. Unfortunately, the recent extended bear market has resulted in considerable losses in these savings plans, and this has adversely affected the retirement plans for many, either resulting in a decision to continue working or to scale back on projected retirement expectations.

Current assessments suggest that the stock market has turned the corner, and while the recovery is expected to be slow, these retirement plans will begin to recover some of the losses incurred over the past three years. In any case, such plans remain the best savings instrument available for retirement, as well as offering a disciplined system to reserve money for later retirement needs on a week-by-week basis. Often the employer matches some portion of these funds deposited from salary. The secret of success in the economics of reserving funds for retirement is financial discipline, and the persons who are conservative in their spending prior to retirement will also continue to be disciplined later. Conversely, those persons who have carried a high level of debt during their productive years will continue to follow the same path after retirement.

For this reason, among others, exploring your financial resources and making any needed adjustments is important in assuring your success after retirement. The major goal is to be debt-free upon reaching retirement, with no outstanding debt, and if possible, arrange your financial planning so that your home mortgage is paid off as well. If you can attain these goals, your only concern will be, hopefully, to keep your living expenses somewhat below your projected income, and to lay aside some savings for those unexpected crises that tend to occur from time to time.

One of the critical factors in financial planning is the need for an exact budget with every possible living expense listed, including housing, utilities (electricity, water, fuel, sewer service, etc.), food, clothing, insurance, transportation, and medical care, also including prescription drug costs. It is very helpful in this process to have each partner to carry a small memo pad, and at the end of each day, list every expenditure made during the day. This process will take no more than five minutes a day. Yet, if you continue it faithfully for a month, you will know exactly what your living expenses are for the month.

Many young couples tell me that they have a budget, but in many cases, their budget has "bleeding ulcers." They realize that a substantial amount of money has been spent, but they have no clue as to where it went. For several years, I taught a class for seniors in the Psychology of Aging, and one of the components was economics for seniors. One elderly couple indicated that they had essentially followed the process outlined above, including a daily record of all expenditures. "In this way, we know what our income will be, and we have a precise list of all of our expenses for the month, and any surplus income we have saved over expenses goes into our "Fooling Around Fund." "They no longer had any need for substantial savings, and any surplus could be used for enjoyment, such as eating out, for the movies, or simply sheer indulgence.

The next subject in the economics of retirement is rapidly becoming a national emergency—the exploding costs of medical care and medical insurance. Because of these escalating costs, and the continuing economic slump, Medicare is reducing its coverage for retirees, as well as reducing the standard payment to doctors. One result of this trend is the number of doctors who are opting out of Medicare and Medicaid service. Another factor in this same concern is the alarming number of highly respected doctors and surgeons who are leaving high-risk fields, such as gynecology and some fields of surgery, because of the prohibitive cost of malpractice insurance. It is to be devoutly hoped, and it is now considered likely, that Congress will act to limit some of the absurd malpractice awards granted by the courts.

Regardless of any efforts to limit some of the most egregious gouging in terms of escalating medical costs and rates for insurance, medical expenses and prescription drugs will continue to be major items in budgeting for retirement. Indeed, many experts are now declaring that the medical establishment in our country is out of control, and the need for some definitive action by Congress is growing more insistent. Some members of the House and Senate are openly advocating universal medical coverage, similar to that of Canada. However, you may expect that any such move will be vehemently opposed by the medical establishment and the insurers, for this would certainly result in a large measure of government control, and consequently, also in substantial loss of profits by the insurance industry.

In any case, and for the foreseeable future, medical care and prescription costs are the major elements in the budgets of seniors today. While there is some predictability and control where the retiree has some form of medical insurance, a large and growing segment of our older people today have no coverage beyond Medicare, and this is only available to those who are above retirement age. As noted above, the payout by Medicare to doctors and hospitals is being reduced. As a result of these conditions, today many elderly people are forced into a tragic choice between expensive prescription drugs or having adequate food on the table.

When our HMO was canceled, along with thousands of others, we took a drastic step. We took the one-hundred dollar monthly fee charged by the HMO and began our own medical expense program, similar to the plan used by many parents to save money for college for their children. Since we have been blessed with good health, this fund has grown to a substantial figure, and it is under our control, rather than the insurance industry or the medical establishment. If the bear market continues to subside, as many financial experts are predicting, then the hope and expectation is that the interest on such an investment will either keep pace with the rate of inflation, or exceed it.

Another issue for those planning retirement is the matter of the investment of one's time. In my experience, few retirees are able to move from full-time work to full-time retirement without some degree of anxiety, unless one has a specific plan in mind. It is not unusual for an employee in a technical field to retire, and at the same time to be welcomed back to the same firm as a consultant, working two or three days a week. This provides a helpful transition period as well as extra income; while at the same time, the employer has the continued service of a valued employee.

I once had a man who retired after more than thirty years in a position in which he had worked four twelve-hour shifts a week, and sometimes five. Practically speaking, his week was usually spent either working or sleeping. As a consequence, his wife had adjusted to a life generally following her own concerns and interests. When he retired, there was no time of transition, and he had no plan or expectation other than to enjoy freedom from a difficult schedule. The day of retirement was duly celebrated, and they set out to enjoy a new life together.

For two or three weeks, they thoroughly enjoyed themselves. They traveled to visit relatives, and they made several day trips to places of interest. They checked out the new shopping malls and generally made the most of their newfound freedom. However, in a month or so, they had run out of places where they wanted to go, and they were forced back to their own resources. Now, with nothing else of interest to do, the husband began to take an active interest in his wife's program. He began to explain to her how she should plan her day and prepare the meals, along with pointed suggestions as to how she should do the laundry. About the middle of the second month, I received an anguished call from the wife, "Rev., can't you do something to get this man out of my hair? I am beginning to consider either divorce or murder!" This brief vignette is a classic example of the need for careful retirement planning.

With all of our plans for the future after retirement, there is also an inevitable looking back. It is of lesser significance, but there is a concern for most people leaving a lifelong profession or career—there is the (usually private) thought, "What will happen to this important service to which I have given my life and loyalty for thirty or forty years?" There is, of course, the realization that the task, career, or profession will go on. However, just as surely, our pride requires that SOMEWHERE there is at least a small corner left behind by us that will be difficult to fill. May I share with you the following reality check, and the author of this gem is anonymous, to the best of my knowledge:

INDISPENSIBLE

Sometime when you're feeling important,
Sometime when your ego's in bloom,
Sometime when you take it for granted,
You're the best qualified in the room.

Sometime when you feel that your going,
Will leave an unfillable hole,
Just follow this simple instruction,
And see how it humbles your soul.

Take a bucket and fill it with water,
Put your hand in it up to the wrist,
Pull it out, and the hole that's remaining,
Is a measure of how much you'll be missed.

You may splash all you please when you enter,
You may stir up the water galore,
But stop, and you'll find in a minute,
That it looks quite the same as before.

The moral in this quaint example,
Is, just do the best that you can,
Be proud of yourself but remember,
There is no indispensable man

Of all the opportunities that come with retirement, none is more important to our well-being than the gift of time. Through the years, how often we have made the comment, not as an excuse, but an observation, "I don't have the time." Now—quite suddenly—you do have the time. Time to lavish on the family, where it was only a gift of chance before. Time to renew old acquaintances and renew old friendships and perchance, time to reflect on the meaning of it all. Did the poet have it right? "I have measured out my life with coffee spoons." In an introspective moment, we may have time to ponder with Peggy Lee, "Is that all there is?"

Yet, this wistful looking back is only half of the reality. We find ourselves in the position of Dr. Peter Marshall, who spoke of "Standing on the threshold of time," between a past that we cannot change and a future that we can never know. Retirement is nothing less than that. It is a looking back to what we have accomplished over the years, but it is also a looking forward to all that lies before us, with all of its promise and hope.

CHAPTER TEN:

The Final Phase—Aging

We come now to the final phase of our journey of life, a survey of the experience of aging. Despite what we may have heard, or our expectations at this point, aging is not an event that occurs at age 65, 75, or older. Rather, it is a process that begins at our birth and continues uniformly day by day until we die. Our chronological age is only one factor among many others in our experience of aging. For example, most of us know persons who are old at sixty, and others who are still enjoying a rich, full life at eighty. In teaching the Psychology of Aging, I designed the enclosed graphic, which expresses many of the realities of aging. The point at the bottom of the diamond reflects the beginning of life, while the apex at the top symbolizes the end of life. I have arbitrarily selected the age of fifty as the pivotal point at the center of the diamond. While there are some losses before that age, particularly in the physical arena, virtually all of the dynamics of life tend toward growth and development. From birth to fifty, life is incremental. In a similar manner, there is continued growth after fifty, such as intellectual or emotional growth, but beyond that age there is slow, but progressive decline. Life beyond the age of fifty is decremental. At our birth, at the bottom of the diamond, we are helpless and totally dependent. At the top, or the apex, if we live long enough, we are again totally helpless and dependent.

The first imperative in the decremental phase is to be aware of the process, and then, secondly, to resist the closing in of the walls with every ounce of our energy and to offset the effects of aging in every way open to us. In the biological effects of aging, the physical is the most apparent, particularly in the senses. We are acutely aware of the decline of sharpness in our vision and hearing. We become aware that the newsprint seems smaller, and people are not speaking as clearly and distinctly as before. We are not as energetic as in younger years. The stairs seem higher and steeper, and we tire more quickly.

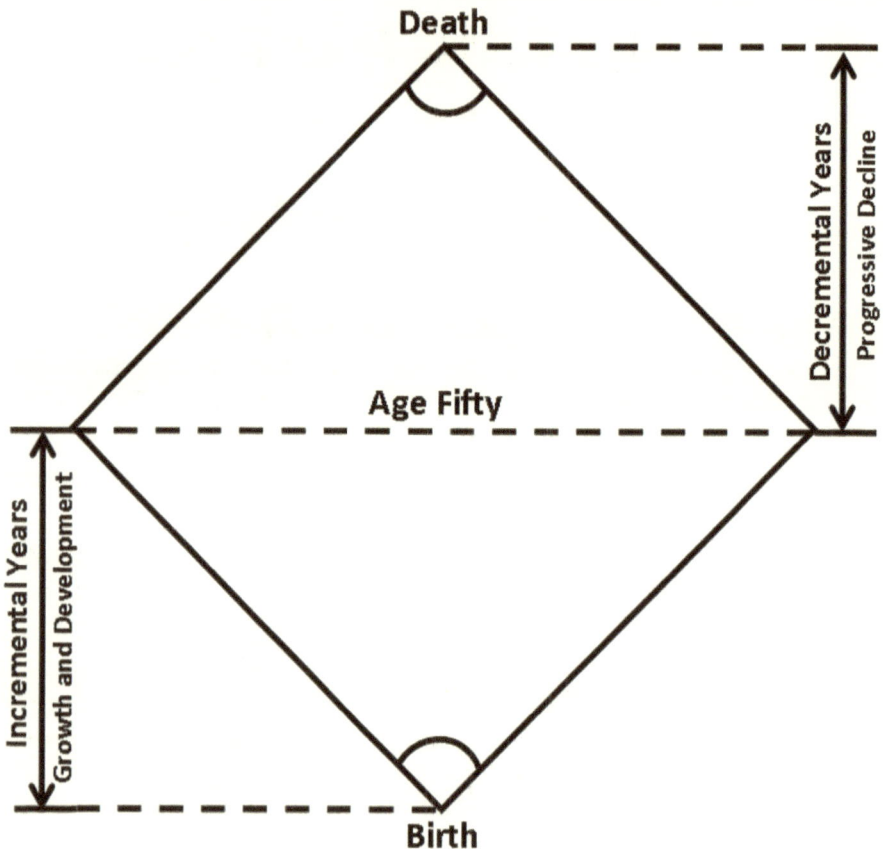

This condition is aggravated by hormonal decline in both men and women, which affects organic function in various ways. Our metabolic rate slows down and despite the fact that we are eating less, we still gain weight because we do not burn calories as we did in an earlier day. This problem is exacerbated further by the fact that we are gradually slowing down in both physical activity and intensity. While we are able to do everything we have done previously, it now seems to require more effort.

A mechanical analogy may be helpful. We buy a new car, and it runs so smoothly and quietly that there is danger of our getting tickets in low-speed zones. However, you take the same car with 100,000 miles on the odometer, and if it has been maintained properly, the steering is fine, the brakes are functioning as they should, and the motor will take you wherever you need to go, but it no longer has the effortless performance we enjoyed at an earlier day. It is the same with our aging bodies. At age sixty or seventy, we can still do most of the things that we did at fifty, but it takes us longer and requires more effort.

The decline in our mental functioning is not as apparent, but it is no less real. The most noticeable loss for most people is short-term memory. We can remember our twelfth birthday party, but we cannot remember where we left our glasses. This whole area of mental function varies rather widely from person to person, but those with the least deficit are usually those who have maintained mental discipline through various interests, such as reading, study in some area of interest, or in working crossword puzzles.

I recall one pastor who retired and fulfilled a lifelong dream by learning New Testament Greek, an interest he had not had time to follow previously. There are some fortunate persons, who remain mentally sharp into advanced old age, but for most of us, some decline in mental functioning must be expected, but also in most cases, it may be compensated for by disciplined mental activity. The old adage applies, "You must use it, or you will lose it."

In both of these areas, the mental and the physical, some regimen of physical activity or exercise seems most productive. Physically, the loss of muscle mass accelerates after we reach fifty, and it becomes more apparent with each decade afterward. However, both the degree and the rate of loss may be slowed substantially by regular activity.

Specialists now tell us that even senior citizens in their 70s and 80s can benefit through the supervised use of weight training and the use of various exercise machines. The experts recommend elevating the pulse rate to the stated maximum for your age and maintaining it for thirty minutes, at least three times a week. In addition to weights and exercise machines, aerobic activity has been proven to be very helpful, with pool aerobics being beneficial for older adults, in particular for those afflicted with various types of arthritis. Such a regimen of guided physical exercise improves muscle tone, improves cardiovascular conditioning, and stimulates blood flow to the brain. In addition to physical enhancement, these activities also generate a feeling of well-being.

Despite the progressive physical decline, a person may continue to grow intellectually, emotionally, and spiritually throughout the lifespan. The value of these various physical improvement programs is dependent upon the discipline of maintaining them. The most common conflict in these regimens is inertia, or the lack of effort and investment in them, or to put it bluntly, the most common problem in this area for many seniors is laziness. Somehow, it seems easier to do nothing than to do something, and it matters little what the something may be. This tendency is insidious, and it tends to be progressive over time, yet it is a one-way ticket to a wheelchair or a vegetative existence.

The flip side to this seductive tendency to inactivity is the elderly person nearing ninety, who walks or exercises faithfully three or more times a week, who keeps an active lifestyle, who enjoys relatively good health, and invests his time in a variety of social and cultural pursuits. His objective is to live until he dies, and in my judgment, that is an attitude that all senior citizens should emulate.

Another common concern that I have observed among our aging population is the tendency to depression. Unfortunately, my impression is that, too often, it is simply seen as a common reflection of aging, and because it is sometimes not diagnosed, it remains untreated. Given the increasing list of aches and pains that come with the advancing years, painful problems with mobility, a constant parade of visits to doctors, dentists, and a variety of clinics, along with the many practical demands of daily living, there is a growing tendency toward withdrawal and isolation, and these merely accentuate the problem. If one effect of depression is seen as turning inward, then a helpful hint in therapy would lie in turning outward. Any kind of activity that encourages the aging person to escape the confines of the home will be beneficial, and if he/she is physically able, any type of volunteer service, such as Meals on Wheels, talking with patients in a nursing home, or any ministry that brings them into regular and creative contact with others will be excellent therapy. A simple act of kindness, such as taking a pot of soup to an elderly shut-in helps to elevate one's mood, and it brightens the day for both the giver and the receiver.

CHAPTER ELEVEN:

The Economics Of Aging

Following physical limitations and health problems, the high cost of prescription drugs and adequate health insurance is next in line for the urgent concern of senior citizens. As noted earlier, many retirees felt reasonably secure in the amount of reserves they had managed to save for the years of aging. Then three years of an almost unprecedented bear market took a heavy toll from their retirement plans and also reduced their expected retirement income drastically.

Now, rather than a relatively secure income, many are reduced to a delicate balancing act between critical health-care costs, rent, or mortgage fees that must be paid, and the daily need for food on the table, then finding that there is never quite enough money to meet even a bare-bones budget. For those who are unable to work, or others who cannot find part-time work, they have found a welcome resource in local senior centers, where a hot meal and welcomed fellowship may be available on most days, for a minimum cost.

Sadly, the great majority of those now in this aging group have raised a family, they have maintained financial independence through years of disciplined management of their money, and now they are on a fixed income and faced with the bleak prospect that they may outlive their finances. For many today, this realization is a constant source of anxiety. On the other hand, for many of these children of the Great Depression, frugal living has been a lifelong habit. They have learned to stock the freezer when local sales occur, shop from store to store to take advantage of weekly specials, and to buy in bulk form when this is practicable. Another source of saving can be realized through the "bundling" of errands, so that several needs may be met through each trip. It is also possible that the few miles driven by such a family could be done at less cost by taking a taxi and avoiding the high cost of owning a car, including insurance and maintenance.

Another important element in the economics of aging is the area of housing. With the empty nest, many parents realize that the three—or four-bedroom house is more than they need at this point in their lives. In most areas today, they are pleasantly surprised to find that the equity in their home has increased substantially over the past decade. Then as they begin to consider a different type of housing, they find a wide variety of options available, from a smaller house to a condominium, an apartment, or an independent living unit in a retirement community. The constant in the whole area of housing is the high cost and the resulting "sticker shock."

While these retirement communities offer a wide range of services, including one to three meals offered for each day, with all forms of support services, often including a health center, the cost for these facilities is quite high, with an entry fee that may be twenty-thousand dollars for a single room, or from fifty-thousand dollars to one-hundred and fifty-thousand dollars for a modest two-room unit or for a small apartment. Then there is an additional maintenance fee that may run as high as four—to five-thousand dollars a month, and any other needed service such as supervision of medications, or help with bathing or dressing, is in addition as well.

For most couples of modest means, most of these options are beyond financial consideration, and as a result, many choose to remain in their own home and continue to cope with increasing maintenance, lawn service, and property taxes that seem to escalate on a regular basis. Other creative housing options include mergers and joint tenancy, in which one no-longer-needed property is sold, and the owner moves in with a friend or relative. Instead of keeping up two large houses, they now share the cost of only one home, substantially reducing the housing costs for each.

A less expensive alternative for some elderly persons lies in moving in with a son or daughter, or other alternative; although in some cases, this may require some addition or other alteration to the home. A major advantage in this solution for a person who requires care is the convenience of on-site management by the care provider. The downside of this arrangement is that it becomes difficult for the caregiver to escape the twenty-four/seven demands of the situation. The ideal is to have other members of the family to step in and provide assistance, as it is needed. However, if such family help is not available, it is absolutely essential for the primary caregiver to have some respite from the daily grind, from some source, at least one day a week to avoid excessive fatigue and emotional burnout and to take care of personal needs.

Moving to a nursing home is usually the last resort when the urgency of the need requires skilled care. These facilities can cost up to five-thousand dollars a month, and often the care received is something less than ideal. Where such a facility is available, a smaller home, providing care for only a few patients, and often owned by a registered nurse, is usually less expensive, and the quality of care is often significantly better. Another advantage is that most of these facilities offer a more home-like lifestyle.

For younger couples in relatively good health who want to downsize, an apartment or a condominium offers freedom from home maintenance and lawn care, along with the many other demands of a private home, including property taxes, all of which helps to conserve money from a fixed income. However, moving from a private home to an apartment or condominium involves a major change in lifestyle. You find yourself living cheek-by-jowl with many other people who may have different schedules from yours (such as a three-to-eleven nurse who runs her vacuum cleaner at 2:00 a.m. in the apartment above you), differing values, and most of all, these persons have little understanding or concern for the meaning of privacy. Such a move to a smaller, but more restrictive, environment may involve a certain degree of social and cultural shock.

Insurance in its many forms is one of the more expensive items in the financial planning of aging persons. Most elderly people have some form of health insurance, but the changing economic climate has led to the bankruptcy of some smaller firms, with the resulting cancellation of health benefits. Sadly, it is not only the smaller firms, but giant corporations as well, as the experience of Bethlehem Steel illustrates. Their retired employees were entitled by contract to health insurance as part of their pension plan, but with the bankruptcy and ultimate sale of Bethlehem Steel, they announced that health-care coverage for their employees would be canceled. This left thousands of their employees scrambling for new coverage, resulting in a drastic and unexpected increase in their budget.

Since virtually all insurance plans today are trying to recover sharply increased costs by raising premiums or reducing coverage, or both, the cost of nursing-home care has escalated to the point that it can wipe out a substantial family estate in one to three years. The insurance firms have recognized this fact, and they have been offering long-term health-care insurance, often including home health care. These plans cover much of nursing-home expenses, but they are so expensive that only relatively wealthy people can afford them. I have been informed by those who have such coverage that their premiums have been raised significantly over the past two years.

MONEY MANAGEMENT AND CRITICAL COSTS

This raises the critical issue of money management. Money management, or financial planning, was unfamiliar or an unknown term a generation ago, except for wealthy people. Now, all of the brokerage houses have financial planning departments, and the level of advertising by these firms, and other specialists in money management, including numerous attorneys now moving into the field, would suggest that there is a ready market among seniors for these services.

While financial firms are largely dealing in investment strategies and portfolio management, attorneys in the field are now offering strategies to avoid probate costs and delays in the settlement of estates, largely through various forms of trusts, along with other legal tactics designed to shield estates from inflated nursing-home costs. All of the above would suggest that these business interests recognize that this group of seniors, as children of the Great Depression era, have traditionally been frugal in their lifestyle, and as a result, they have amassed a large amount of capital now in the process of being passed on to a new generation, and unfortunately, a generation more known for its excesses than through any interest in savings.

As one might expect, the scent of money has spawned a whole new industry seeking to tap into this vast well of cash, now reputed to be the largest single transfer of capital from one generation to another in our history. Many of these businesses are legitimate, seeking market strategies to tap into these reserves. However, many of these schemes offered today range from the marginal to outright scams, deliberately designed to exploit trusting seniors.

These scams range from "Investment Opportunities" to offers for home improvements, such as roofing and siding, cleaning gutters, or sealing driveways, usually asking for most (or all) of the money up front for material, etc.—and, if cash is given, they are gone, with no intention to do the work promised. It should be noted that these scams, and often telemarketing schemes, are based on the assumption that older persons are more trusting, and in many cases because of this trait, they may become easy targets. In one recent case in Baltimore, an unscrupulous contractor had done over one hundred thousand dollars worth of work on the row house of a widow. A municipal inspector sent out in response to a newspaper story of the incident found that the little work that was actually done ranged from shoddy to worthless. When the court found the contractor liable, he promptly declared bankruptcy.

A note of caution should be sounded at this point. The victims of such frauds are not always just trusting or gullible. These operators are so polished and the schemes they offer seem so legitimate that well-educated and responsible people, and even established business leaders, are also victimized. From vacation trips offered, to investments that promise high dividends, common sense would suggest that if it sounds too good to be true, it probably is too good to be true.

What should aging people do with their surplus funds? Numerous stories can be told of persons losing their life savings in the Bank Holiday of the 1930s who thereafter distrusted banks. In many cases, the family repository was under the mattress. It was reported that one farmer was known for his penchant of taking extra cash in silver dollars, then secretly dropping them into his well. They were safe for sure! Another recent example of a restaurant owner who also distrusted banks, kept his money at home. A couple of enterprising crooks either knew of his habit, or suspected it, found his home address and waited in hiding until he returned home. They confronted the owner with guns and robbed him of over two hundred and fifty thousand dollars in cash. Fortunately, through some good police work, the criminals were apprehended, but as usual, the money was not recovered.

For most retired people, we want the best return on our savings that is available to us. The cardinal rule in investing is that the level of risk is directly related to the level of return, and the higher the level of return, the higher the risk. A second general rule is that we should reduce our exposure to loss in relation to our age. This suggests that following retirement, a higher percentage of our savings should be in investments in which the principle is guaranteed, such as certificates of deposit, or carefully selected bonds. Among the latter, many seniors favor municipal bonds, particularly those that are tax-exempt.

It would appear that the bear market is slowly receding, and seniors who have suffered serious losses in their retirement funds have been reluctant to return to the market. Since the stock market always poses some level of risk, some financial specialists suggest that the key question should be, "How much can I afford to lose?" The premise seems to be that if you have reserves that you really do not need at this point, then it is reasonable to assume that you may invest those funds for future growth.

In terms of money management, a common question for many aging persons is their fear of becoming incapacitated. "What happens if I have a heart attack or suffer a stroke that renders me incapable of functioning?" This is a real concern that affects anyone approaching elderly status. Many wills affecting couples are written on a complimentary basis. That means that when the first spouse dies, all proceeds of the estate revert to the surviving spouse, who then becomes responsible for the management of the estate. At this point the question becomes critical. With increasing age, health questions are a logical concern, but an even greater question is raised by the fear of possible incompetence.

The medical solution to this fear is the Living Will, or the Advanced Directive, by which one may direct the procedures to be followed in case of a catastrophic event. There are also practical questions to be answered in regard to daily decisions. This need may be resolved by granting some form of Power of Attorney to a spouse, or a trusted family member. This allows the person selected to act in your place, making needed decisions, signing checks, or whatever actions may be required. A cause of concern is that in many cases, the person chosen is in total control of your life and assets. For these reasons, this course of action should only be taken through the advice and counsel of a trusted attorney.

We come now to the final chapter in the survey of the family, when the hand of time grows heavy upon us. I have talked with many aging people about their thoughts and feelings at this point in their pilgrimage in life. For the great majority, there is the feeling that they have been blessed with the gift of a longer life, a life in which they have learned important lessons from their mistakes and failures, and through it all, the flood of memories are far more good than bad, and where levels of growing may yet be anticipated. Robert Browning, in his poem, Rabbi Ben Ezra, expresses these feelings:

> I'm growing fonder of my staff,
> I'm growing dimmer in my eyes,
> I'm growing fainter in my laugh,
> I'm growing deeper in my sighs,
> I'm growing careless of my dress,
> I'm growing frugal of my gold,
> I'm growing wise, I'm growing—
> Yes! I'm growing old.

CHAPTER TWELVE:

The Fears Of Aging

For a generation who saw two great wars, one that has been called "The Greatest Generation," by objective observers, and a generation that took great pride in their self-sufficiency, it is not surprising that the most common fear in this age group lies in the fear of losing their independence. The fear most commonly expressed is the fear of losing their sight or hearing, perhaps because they are most aware of growing deficits in those areas. A second problem is also related to the problems of advancing years, the fear of losing mobility, of being reduced to a cane or a walker. In all of these concerns, the real anxiety is derived from the fear of becoming dependent upon others for the basic needs of life. You will recall the graphic in the form of a diamond, with infancy, or the beginning of life, at the bottom point. Most aging persons are acutely aware of the closing in of the walls in the second half of their lives, and the potential just ahead, of a second infancy at the apex of the diamond, in which, once again, they may be completely helpless and dependent.

The first major step in this direction is the critical point at which family members, or the family doctor, announce regretfully that you must surrender your driver's license. It may well be that you have not driven more than two—or three-thousand miles in the past year. However, that driver's license and the ignition keys in your pocket are symbols of freedom, and the loss is devastating, not only in the practical sense, but even more in the implications for the future, the progressive loss of independence.

All aging persons fear some crippling injury that will result in further loss of independence. For diabetics, there is the progressive fear of the loss of sight, and the possible loss of a limb, a foot, or a leg, through amputation. When you pursue the fear, it is not so much the practical adjustments one must make in order to manage the functions of daily life, but rather the permanence of such a loss. It is forever, and there is no way to compensate for it. I believe that for many seniors, one of the more difficult losses is the gradual erosion of the sense of self, or our self-image. We are conscious that we are not as competent, either physically or mentally, as we once were. With the wrinkles of age and the waning of energy, we do not feel that we are as attractive or as interesting as we once were.

These thoughts bring us to the mental and emotional aspects of aging. As noted previously, there is an unconscious tendency to withdraw, to retreat from a world that seems more and more insecure for us. With the loss of energy, there is a tendency toward neglect of our surroundings, to spend less time in keeping our home or room clean and neat. Because we are reluctant to go out, less attention is paid to our dress and appearance. However, if we surrender to these subtle temptations to lessened activity, depression in some degree is almost certain to follow.

How shall we respond to these inner conflicts that rob us of energy, and the loss of enjoyment in our lives? I believe that the key word is attitude. We are realistic enough to understand our limitations, but we also should be aware that there are almost limitless possibilities for growth and learning that lie before us, if we are willing to invest our time and energy to make it happen. A crucial comment is attributed to Jack Benny, "Aging is simply mind over matter; if you don't mind, it doesn't matter."

The importance of attitude is reflected in an experience that I had in visiting a patient in a hospital. A staff doctor came in, and after some conversational small talk, he gently informed her that she had a form of cancer that was inoperable and terminal. There were momentary tears, followed by matter-of-fact questions regarding continuing procedures. Finally, the doctor asked how she was feeling, and she replied with a question, "Doctor, I am not going to die today, am I?" and the doctor replied, "No, of course not." Without a moment of hesitation, the patient responded, "Then I am going to live today!" Inside, I wanted to stand up and cheer.

I recall a similar experience that I had with a friend who had been a diabetic for much of his adult life. He had been struggling with painful ulcers in his feet with almost constant infection. When gangrene developed, his doctor informed him that he no longer had a choice, that he must have both feet amputated, and that it was likely that he would be confined to a wheelchair. He considered this for a moment then he asked, "Will you be able to fit me with prostheses?" The doctor thought about this, then he answered that he believed that he was a suitable candidate for prostheses. My friend replied, "Then I will not only be walking, but in six months, I will also be dancing!" True to his word, he worked diligently in the rehab process, and in the six months promised, he was indeed able to dance.

A thoughtful person asked the question, "How are aging people different from others?" The answer is that aging persons are just like other people, only more so! As we grow older, the old-timers once said that we become set in our ways. In other words, the aging process seems to heighten personality traits or characteristics. The one who is temperamental in middle age will become more so at eighty. The person who is ego-centered and selfish in earlier days will be even more inclined to act this way in later years. Most of us have observed that a person who "enjoys ill health" at fifty will also complain endlessly about his aches and pains, as he grows older. However, the opposite is true as well. A person who is generous and giving in his adult years will also be openhanded and openhearted at eighty.

In my opinion, no single word seems to identify a person so much as attitude. I knew one lady who lived alone and remained independent until she was past one-hundred years of age. If her kitchen needed to be brightened, she would get out her stepladder and wash it down, just as she had done for the past fifty years. She loved the monthly women's fellowship at her church, and she continued to make her famed baked-bean recipe for their luncheons. As a result of her positive attitude, she enjoyed her life almost until her death at one hundred and three.

You may recall the story of George Burns, who announced that he had signed a contract to play the Palladium in London on his one-hundredth birthday! He is also reputed to have made the observation, "If I had known that I would live so long, I would have taken better care of myself!" Bishop Herbert Welsh, who holds the record as the most senior United Methodist Bishop, expressed a similar attitude. He lived to be one-hundred-and-five years old. He was a most exceptional man, endowed with a quick wit and a mind that remained sharp until his death. A reporter was interviewing him on his one hundred and fifth birthday and asked him, "Bishop Welsh, you have been a keen observer of life for more than a century. What would you believe to be the most important year in your life?" Without a moment's hesitation, the Bishop replied, "The next one!" That is the sort of positive attitude that we need to develop and maintain with the wisdom of advancing years.

Similarly, I had an acquaintance who lived into her mid-nineties, whose sight had deteriorated until she was legally blind, yet her faculties remained sharp until she died. She listened to national and international news daily, and she had an informed opinion in world affairs, both politically and diplomatically. She maintained contact with her many friends by telephone, and it was reported that you could give her your name and telephone number, and a week later, she could recall your number and call you by name. It would seem that most people could maintain sharp mentality by concentrating on intellectual activities that stimulate mental functioning.

One of the more difficult issues that every person must work through emotionally, both for the aging and for others, is the inner strength to cope with losses. Fortunately, this is a lifelong process that begins for most of us in childhood, when your goldfish or hamster dies, or your kitten is killed by a car, and you begin to develop the resources we need to cope with the pain of loss. Our experience of the loss of relationships deepens when a dear childhood friend moves away to another state. These losses in relationships are progressive, and each loss that we encounter helps to endow us with more emotional strength to deal with the next.

Every person will encounter many losses in a lifetime. A teenager feels the loss of self in their first identity crisis, and out of that painful experience, they are better prepared to deal with the concerns of life. A housewife, and mother, finds a second identity crisis in her final encounter with the empty nest when the last child leaves home. "If I am not a mother, who am I?" Many others, both male and female, find that they must redefine themselves after they retire, since almost everyone finds some validation in their work.

For aging persons, these losses seem to be clustered in three broad categories—the physical, the material, and the relational. Physical losses include the loss of youth and sexual vitality, the waning of physical strength, the deterioration in sight and hearing, and the progressive loss of mobility. Surely, one of the most painful of these losses is the loss of independence. Material losses may occur at any time, but they surely come in the reduction of income through retirement, with the resultant deterioration in lifestyle that this requires of most of us, and the constant effort to bridge the gap between constantly rising costs and a fixed income. Material losses are reflected in the escalation in the cost of health care, not only in visits to doctors and hospitals, but also in the alarming increase in the cost of prescription drugs.

Relational losses for the aging are most clearly seen in the annual family reunions, with the counting of the seats that have become empty since the last gathering. With these experiences, there is a growing sense of mortality, with the hands of time becoming more apparent with each passing year. Along with these symbols of aging, there comes the realization that you have outlived so many of your relatives and friends. At the same time, you are aware that you have experienced so many of the joys of living and amassed a lifetime of fond memories. The final realization is that each of these years beyond the Biblical three-score and ten is a special gift of grace.

Our experience of the ultimate relational loss through death usually begins with the death of a grandparent, often by the time we are ten or twelve years old, followed by the deaths of uncles or aunts. An occasional tragedy may claim the life of a brother or sister, or even a parent, at a relatively young age. By the teen years, and certainly as young adults, we have normally observed death sufficiently to enable us to begin to see death in the context of life. Young persons may die, but old people must die. To the observant, we may learn of the death of a grandparent, and within a few days, we celebrate the birth of a new baby in the family system. This helps us to understand death as a normal and natural part of the rhythm of life.

To young persons, teenagers and younger, death is an incomprehensible enigma, absolutely foreign to the natural exuberance and vitality of youth. It is common, in my experience, to find a teenager who refuses to attend a funeral, even of a close relative, or to enter a funeral home. The ongoing experiences of life tend to lead us through and beyond these irrational but natural human fears with the passing of the years and with the gains and losses of living.

One of the most commonly expressed fears of aging is the fear of becoming a victim. Since the current aging population has been the most frugal and the most dedicated group in our history to "save for the future," all of that available cash has become an irresistible target for scam artists with a hundred creative schemes to separate the elderly from their money. Since the recent bear market has been so devastating for seniors, as well as others, a new twist has emerged, which offers to recover the losses we have suffered in the stock market over the past three years, for an up-front fee, of course. Don't go for this one.

Seniors, as well as others, are deluged with telemarketers, and the use of e-mail for those who have computers, offering a wide variety of "unusual investment opportunities," with the promise of high returns on your investment. The wisest resource in these situations is common sense. If it sounds too good to be true, it probably is too good to be true. An arbitrary rule should be observed at this point. NEVER go to a bank and withdraw any substantial amount of money without first conferring with an attorney, a trusted financial consultant, or even the bank manager, in order to obtain an objective opinion regarding the venture. If it appears to be questionable in any degree, then avoid it.

Experiences such as the following abound in our day. An elderly husband had died and left the family estate to his wife. Since she was left alone in a large house, her only son suggested that he and his family move in with her to take care of her for the rest of her life, with the assumption that the property would come to him upon her death. These arrangements were finalized, and a year later, the son came to her with a request. He was involved in a business deal in which he needed some equity. Could she sign over the property in his name? She reasoned that the property would go to him eventually, so why not now? She signed over the deed as requested, and in less than a year, she was moved out of her home into an assisted living facility, where her assets were soon liquidated.

A new version of the old "Pigeon Drop" has surfaced recently. In this ploy, an elderly woman was approached outside of a mall, and she was told that the scammer had found a lottery ticket worth millions, and she could have a substantial share if she could produce some "earnest money." Since she was on a fixed and limited income, she was excited by the lure of some extra money. She went with her new friends to her bank where she withdrew $15,000 from her account. When the friends informed her that this was not enough, she took them to her home where she gave them $2,000 more in cash and several thousand dollars worth of jewelry. The crooks then drove her back to the mall where she was to receive her windfall and they promptly disappeared. These criminals were never identified, and no arrest was ever made in her unfortunate situation.

In most areas, the "bank examiner" scam surfaces frequently. In this scam, the victim receives a phone call that her bank suspects that a bank officer is skimming funds and they need the victim's help in setting up a sting. The scam is authenticated by official phone calls from the bank manager, who of course, is an accomplice. The victim is instructed to withdraw a specific amount from her account, and these bills are then marked and supposedly replaced in the account. Instead, it promptly disappears with the perpetrators. In this case, as in so many others, a two-minute conference with the real bank manager would have derailed the scheme and thus saved the money involved.

Another common crime against the elderly involves criminals coming to the door with fake uniforms and badges. When they are admitted, they rob the residents of all the cash and other valuables they can locate quickly, and in a matter of minutes, they are gone. Some of these scam artists have stated that they are from Social Security and that an overpayment has been made in the account of the victim, usually of several hundred dollars. The "Investigators" tell the victim that the stated amount must be refunded in cash or their Social Security checks will be stopped. Vulnerable persons need to know that the Social Security Administration NEVER operates in this manner.

In almost all of these crimes against the aging, the victim is warned that he/she must not tell anyone, that absolute secrecy must be maintained. This in itself raises a huge red flag that something is seriously amiss. Some of these scams are based on the premise that somehow you can get something for nothing, which is another caution flag. One of the major assumptions used by those who exploit the elderly is that persons of this age group grew up in a world of trust, where a handshake was the only contract made, because a man's word was his bond. So the crooks say to the aging, "This is a great deal! Trust me!"

Fair warning must be given also that these individuals and companies that practice these criminal activities are so sophisticated and plausible in their schemes that they are usually successful, and they are seldom apprehended. Also, these plots are so clever and complex that even skilled lawyers and executives are victimized. A classic example of the complexity of some of these financial frauds is the case of the bank executive who managed foreign currency transactions. He was so familiar with the complex system of records, and he possessed such encyclopedic knowledge of the checks and balances, that he was able to escape detection until he had lost more than five million dollars of the bank's funds. He was able to escape detection, not only for a few weeks or months, but also for years.

CHAPTER THIREEN:

The Closing Chapter

In considering the fears of aging, it is surprising to some researchers in the field to find that there is little fear of dying among elderly people. There is, of course, the realization that time runs on, and one day it will run out. In Frank Sinatra's great hit, "September Song," we find the line, "And so I face the final curtain." I suspect that every person in the closing years of life who is mentally alert will spend some time in evaluating his/her pilgrimage of life, and in that process, they will wonder how the book of life will close for them. However, death is like taxes—its certainty is never in doubt. You may recall the line from a country and western song and the line that reminds us, "You will never get out of this world alive."

The wisdom of Ecclesiastes speaks poetically of the time when "The silver cord be broken, or the pitcher be broken at the fountain, or the wheel be broken at the cistern. Then shall the dust return to the earth as it was, and the spirit shall return to God, who gave it." In any case, it is a profound experience, the final period at the end of the last sentence.

A convict on Death Row, who was to be executed the next day, requested to see the warden. As one might expect, the dialogue was difficult for both. Finally, the condemned man asked what was going to happen to him. The warden misinterpreted the question and assured the man that his family would pick up the body and make the final arrangements as desired. The convict exploded in exasperation, "I don't care about that, but where will I be after you pull that switch tomorrow?"

The convict was expressing the ultimate question that must be asked by every dying person.

Many people live their lives with little thought about the meaning of faith, but as death approaches, they have no choice, because death is a journey from which no traveler ever returns. Death is the final mystery, which every person must ponder. Whether a heavenly existence and eternal life, or the Hindu concept of reincarnation where life is conceived to be an endless cycle of rebirths, or as a spiritual presence among family and friends, the vast majority of people conceive of some level of being or existence beyond death. Neil Diamond's positive assertion, "I am, I said, I am, I cried," is a declaration of being, and the thought of non-being, or extinction, seems foreign and unacceptable to us.

The most anxious concern among most elderly persons seems to revolve around the manner of our passing, with the ideal being to die in one's sleep, as the most preferable, followed by a catastrophic stroke or a massive heart attack. In any case, we are social creatures, and we need each other. The one universal concern that I have found is the fear of dying alone; we want someone with us when we take that final step. In my experience of fifty years, when an option is possible, most people prefer to die at home in familiar surroundings, among family and friends. Most seem willing to accept a higher level of discomfort and perhaps less professional care to make this possible. I have shared the final days and hours with many persons over the years, and a surprising number were sufficiently aware of impending death to express their final farewells.

Dr. Elisabeth Kubler-Ross, an eminent psychiatrist who recently died, did the original research and provided us with her definitive study of death in her best-selling book published in 1969, "On Death and Dying." The motivation for her work was the need to provide greater understanding of the process and to surround our experience of death with dignity, peace, and every measure of comfort and security available to us.

While I believe that there is a substantial difference in the process of death in a person dying at eighty, having lived a full life, and another dying of Lou Gehrig's disease at fifty, there are several common denominators that most dying persons will pass through. Dr. Kubler-Ross identifies five such stages, the first being denial, in which the person is either unwilling or unable to accept the reality of dying. When the certainty of death can no longer be denied, the second stage is anger: "Why is this happening to me? This is not fair!" The third stage is bargaining for more time, and when it becomes apparent that this hope is failing, the fourth stage is depression. In time, with growing understanding, and surrounded by emotional and spiritual support, the fifth stage of acceptance is reached.

As noted above, the thought of extinction or non-being is unacceptable to us, and there is the stubborn conviction within us that there is something beyond. This denoted some level of faith, and beyond this faith there is hope. As Dr. Kubler-Ross said in confronting her own death, "I am going to dance in all of the galaxies."

THE FUNERAL

Since every family must deal with funerals, a word regarding death and the funeral arrangements may be helpful. In a manner that may seem surprising to some, a growing number of aging persons want to plan their own funeral. This would include the selection of a funeral home, personal choice of a casket, the selection of a minister to officiate, and the burial site. In most of these cases, the complete funeral service is planned, including the hymns desired and the familiar Scriptures to be read. In most cases, the cemetery and the gravesite have been selected in advance. Incidentally, many funeral homes today are offering advance planning, including prepayment of the entire cost. While this provides some assurance to the aging person, and it relieves the family of making difficult choices at the time of death, such prepayment is not usually the most practical solution economically.

Secondly, a growing number of families today are choosing cremation as an alternative to the high cost of a traditional funeral. Some cemeteries will permit the burial of a funerary urn atop an existing family gravesite. Also, as a result of shrinking space available, aboveground crypts are increasing rapidly, not only in the typical mausoleums, but also in individual aboveground crypts. While such private crypts were once the symbols of a wealthy family, the individual or dual crypts are now seen in every large cemetery.

While large corporations have acquired many cemeteries and funeral homes in the "funeral business" purely for profit, the vast majority of funeral homes continue to provide a sensitive and caring ministry to bereaved families. One such funeral home with which I have been associated for many years, the J.J. Hartenstein Mortuary in New Freedom, PA, offers the services of a trained bereavement counselor as well as an annual service of remembrance for the families of those who have died in the previous year. This family-owned funeral home is in their fourth generation.

The funeral service itself has changed dramatically over the years since World War II. Up until then, it was common practice to hold the "wake" and the funeral service in the family home. The term "wake" was well chosen since the family and friends sat in the room with the deceased through the night. While some may see the funeral as morbid and depressing, the whole process has been very carefully designed to assist the family in the grieving process.

In the customary one—or two-day "viewing" with the deceased lying in state, the grieving person (or family) must repeatedly recite the details of the person's death. Often, the visitor was close enough to the deceased that the grief they express will also reopen the well of tears of the spouse or family member as they weep together. This experience stimulates and encourages the grieving experience. Occasionally, one may find a spouse or a close relative who does not weep and seems unperturbed. In most cases, this suggests some level of denial. However, we must remember that the grief work, as it has been termed, may be delayed, but it cannot be denied, and it must be experienced sooner or later.

In one extreme situation, the body of a husband was partially incinerated in the explosion and fire of a gasoline tanker truck. The funeral, of necessity, was held with a closed casket. This circumstance led to serious problems for the wife, expressing some questions about her husband's death, ultimately resulting in her denial of the whole process, adamantly insisting that her husband was just away. Obviously, this was an extreme condition requiring professional intervention. Such a response is not unusual, however, in tragedies such as the World Trade Towers' disaster, or when a body is lost at sea.

With the growing popularity of cremation services and in other cases in which it may be appropriate, the memorial service may be held at a different time from the interment. This separation makes it possible to schedule the memorial service at the most opportune time when out-of-town guests have time to plan ahead and travel arrangements can be made in advance. Such services allow for more careful planning including preparation for various persons to speak about the life and times of the deceased. This separation also provides more of an opportunity to present a broader perspective of the background of the person as well as a fuller expression of the celebration of the life of the person to be memorialized. Such a service usually includes a carefully selected series of photographs reflecting the life of the deceased, as well as verbal anecdotes offered by selected speakers. This is usually accomplished through a carefully arranged set of photographs celebrating various experiences from his/her life.

The funeral service or memorial service will vary somewhat reflecting the faith community represented, but ideally, it has a dual focus as suggested above—mourning a death, but to an even greater degree, you are celebrating a life. The personality of the deceased is remembered, recalling the interests and other pursuits he/she enjoyed, the personal hobbies or other activities that were important, particularly the family relationships, the children, grandchildren, and great grandchildren, since typically, their greatest joy and fulfillment is found in these family relationships. This becomes even more critical with the progressive limitations that come with age.

I recall one particularly poignant experience in which an aging father was largely confined to a comfortable lounge chair during the day. In this case, the family dog was his constant companion, often just lying at his feet. After his death and for several days following, the dog would sit on the floor and look up at the empty chair, as though he could not comprehend the absence of his friend.

The most difficult experience for the surviving spouse, or for the family, occurs with the first sight of the husband or wife in the funeral home with the open casket in which the reality of the loss becomes almost overwhelming. The second most painful event comes with the closing of the casket, either before the funeral service, or at its conclusion, in which the finality of the separation must be accepted.

Our human response to this level of grief will vary, sometimes to the extreme. In one situation, the widow had the family come in on the day after the funeral, and at her insistence, they removed all of her husband's clothing as well as everything that he had owned. Every vestige of his presence was removed, and the home was left as if he had never existed. In the second case, in a totally opposite reaction, in a year following her husband's death, nothing related to her husband had been touched. His clothing and the other objects he had used were kept just as he left them, including his pipe left in the ashtray where he had laid it aside. In each of these cases, the counselor will recognize that an unusual problem is being presented, a problem that must be explored in the ministry offered following the funeral.

Rather regularly, people will ask about the choice between cremation and the traditional funeral. One of the problems to be considered is the disposition of the remains. If the ashes are scattered, as is often the case, then there is no gravesite where one may continue the grieving process. As noted previously, some cemeteries will allow the burial of the urn atop the existing grave of a family member, which provides a specific place to visit. This need is also provided for by those cemeteries with mausoleums, which offer niches for crematorial urns. Finally, with the differing costs set aside, the question becomes one of preference, or convenience.

Since death is universal, philosophers and poets have examined it extensively. An earlier American poet, William Cullen Bryant, in his poem, "Thanatopsis," provides a fitting closure.

> So live that when thy summons comes to join the innumerable caravan which moves to that mysterious realm, where each must take his place in the silent halls of death, go thou not as the quarry slave at night, scourged to his dungeon, but sustained and soothed by an unfaltering trust, approach thy grave, like one who wraps the drapery of his couch about him and lies down to pleasant dreams.

Or this brief poem, "Well Done," by James Montgomery:

> Servant of God, well done! Rest from thy loved employ;
> The battle fought, the victory won, enter thy Master's joy.
> The pains of death are past, labor and sorrow cease,
> And life's long warfare closed at last, thy soul is found in peace.

A Biblical vision of the life to come is found in The Revelation, fittingly, the last chapter of the Bible (Chapter 21). "And I John, saw the holy city, New Jerusalem, coming down from God out of heaven, prepared as a bride adorned for her husband. And I heard a great voice out of heaven saying, "The house of God is with men, and He will dwell with them, and they shall be His people, and God, Himself, shall be with them, and be their God. And God shall wipe away the tears from their eyes, and there shall be no more death, neither sorrow nor crying, and neither shall there be any more pain, for all of the former things are passed away." And He that sat upon the throne said, "Behold, I make all things new." "That newness visions a time when the pains of life all have ended, the tears of life have all been shed. Death has been overcome with victory and the worn-out body is laid aside like last week's discarded clothing. This reality is reflected in the great old country standard, "This Old House:"

> "Ain't gonna need this house no longer, ain't gonna need this
> house no more;
> Got no time to oil the hinges, got no need to fix the floor."

We shall have a new body, no cancer, no arthritis, no need for artificial joints, a new body for a new life that will endure forever.

It is fitting that we close with remembrance of a tragic death during the Civil War. You may recall that General "Stonewall" Jackson was one of the most valiant and trusted of the commanders of General Robert E. Lee's Confederate army. He was returning to camp in the dusk of the early evening. For some reason, never quite clear, he was not recognized by a sentry and accidentally shot. Given the primitive medicine at the time, there was little to be done, and General Jackson died within a few days. Shortly before he died, he wrote the following prayer and gave it to a chaplain who included it in a book I was fortunate enough to acquire.

> "Master, Lord, bestow thy benediction; quiet our fevered
> hearts; grant us thy peace and thy joy. Then Lo! in every duty
> laid on our hands, in the face of every friend, in the need of
> every brother man I can help, in all the good I can do, I shall
> find here my Promised Land. And there, in that country to
> come, in that continuing City whose builder and Maker is
> God, we shall take off our dusty shoes, throw away our worn
> staff and our soiled garments, and salute the Lord, and greet

the saints, and be at rest over the river, under the shade of the trees, in the Promised Land of God."

So we conclude this study of family life, from the cradle to the grave, trusting that people struggling with the stresses and strains and the complexity of family life today, with its many conflicts and the constant ambiguities, may find some practical hints and resources in the material presented. Trusting that the good will always outweigh the evil, and that joys and fulfillments will be greater than the frustrations and the problems, and rejoice in the end, "That God sets the solitary apart in families."

As I was preparing the Chapter headings as requested, I suddenly realized that my book was not finished. The personal history of an individual indeed closes with the person's death and subsequent funeral, but the family history continues until the estate is settled, and this often proves to be the most contentious and divisive process in the life history of the family. This material is presented as an addendum.

CHAPTER FOURTEEN:

The Addendum:
The Settlement Of The Estate

One of the critical factors in the settlement of the estate is the family structure. Was there only one child, or two or more? The process is less complex with an only child, where the bulk of the estate will almost certainly go to the only heir.

In other situations where there are multiple offspring, one of the issues confronted by the surviving spouse is the equitable distribution of the estate. Another significant factor in many of these family histories revolves around the question as to who was most responsible in the care of the aging parents. As noted earlier, one of the children will usually emerge as the one most responsible, and that person will become the primary caregiver, and it is not necessarily the firstborn or the youngest. Often it is a daughter, but it may be a son.

Proximity plays a role here as well, with the sibling who lives nearest being expected to be most available, but not always. I knew of one case in which the primary caregiver was not a daughter, but a daughter-in-law, who lived eighty-five miles away. In the last year of the life of her mother-in-law, she made the one-hundred-and-seventy mile round-trip two or three times a week to provide transportation to doctors or clinics, to grocery stores, or to pick up prescriptions. Other family members lived much closer, but they were too busy, or it was otherwise inconvenient for them.

Occasionally, we find a family in which each of the children are able to share in the care of aging parents regularly, but this is not usually the case. Where the responsible one is meeting the need, the other siblings are too busy, or they have young children, or they live too far away. The irrational factor often seen in the settlement of estates is that, almost without exception, those family members, who have contributed little or nothing in the care of an aging mother or father, expect an equal share of the estate.

In my own family, when our parents aged to the extent that they were no longer able to live independently, my younger sister moved in with them and remained as the primary caregiver until both had died. While others lived at some distance from the parental home, each came in for an occasional night or a weekend, in order to provide some respite for the primary caregiver. Upon the death of my mother, each family member gladly signed off on the estate, recognizing gratefully that our younger sister had earned the inheritance through her years of sacrificial service in the care of our parents.

However, having noted the high incidence of family battles over an estate (and having served as the referee for several), what possibility do we have that these unfortunate family squabbles may be avoided, or at least reduced? Given the percentage of self-centered persons in our world, as compared to the world of their parents, I am not optimistic. But in the interest of fairness, we should observe that these people did not choose to be the way they are. Throughout their younger lives, most of them have been surrounded by abundance. As a consequence, I have seen children playing in a room filled with toys, yet they are complaining, "Mama, I'm bored!" This scenario tends to produce high maintenance people, and "Enough" is not in their vocabulary.

I have seen cases after the death of the last parent that one or more of the children enter the home immediately after the funeral, and help themselves to various family treasures, without the knowledge or consent of other family members, often beginning with the family silver, or other valuable artifacts.

Given human nature, I suspect that it is unrealistic to hope that such selfish behavior may be prevented. However, it may be substantially reduced by carefully designating in the will the chosen recipient of each article of value from the family possessions. Some seniors unwittingly contribute to the problem in attempting to economize through drawing up their own will, perhaps using a form found on the Internet. Unless the conditions are exceptionally simple, this is seldom a good idea. If there is sufficient estate to merit a will, the modest cost of having the will drawn up legally by an attorney will surely be justified, and if there are minefields in the conditions to be carried out, these may be identified and addressed with such legal clarity that litigation or questioning of the will becomes unlikely.

Additional insurance to preclude these family hassles may be derived from making the provisions of settlement of the estate as fair and equitable as circumstances permit. In such cases where the caregiver is to be rewarded by a larger share of the estate, the rationale and the specific terms should be clearly stated, either in the will or in a legal codicil.

A final observation may be made relative to life in the family. If the parents have been scrupulously fair in the early years in the family, both in the relationship to each other, and with the children, then the proper traits of character such as honesty and fairness, carefully modeled by their parents, will likely be emulated by their children, and the anger and resentment often seen, may be avoided.

To paraphrase Rabbi Kushner, bad things may happen to good people. However, I believe that if the last parent to die, either father or mother, has been loved and respected through seventy-five or more years of life, it is likely that the memory of that respect will be observed by their adult children, and the love shared in the family circle will become the dominant reality in the settlement of the estate.

www.ingramcontent.com/pod-product-compliance
Lightning Source LLC
Chambersburg PA
CBHW030359290526
45785CB00004B/1816